Christmas Evans—
no ordinary preacher
The story of the 'John Bunyan'
of Wales

Tim Shenton

DayOne

© Day One Publications 2008
First printed 2008

ISBN 978–1–84625–130–6

British Library Cataloguing in Publication Data available

Published by Day One Publications
Ryelands Road, Leominster, HR6 8NZ
☎ 01568 613 740 FAX 01568 611 473
email—sales@dayone.co.uk
web site—www.dayone.co.uk
North American—e-mail—sales@dayonebookstore.com
North American—web site—www.dayonebookstore.com

Cover design by Wayne McMaster
Printed by Gutenberg Press, Malta

Commendations on Tim Shenton's larger work on Christmas Evans (Christmas Evans: The life and times of the one-eyed preacher of Wales), *on which this book is based, include:*

'This book truly warms the heart and is a timely reminder of what the Lord can do through the simple preaching of the gospel.'

Evangelical Presbyterian Magazine

'Tim Shenton has done Baptists and the Church of Jesus Christ a great favour in producing this new and definitive biography.'

The Baptist Page

'A well researched and excellent biography … a spiritually uplifting work.'

Peace and Truth

'Tim Shenton's extensive, thorough and well-documented research has produced the most accurate work on Christmas Evans that has ever appeared; it is certainly going to be the standard work for many years to come. It is written in a style everyone can enjoy, and with a spiritual insight that makes every page worthwhile.'

Stuart Olyott, former pastor, author and speaker, UK

Contents

Contents

Wiliam Edwards gives high praise when he says, 'Christmas Evans was a Paul in labour, a Bunyan in imagination, and a Whitefield in eloquence. He stood on the highest pinnacle of fame as a preacher; but more than this—his record is on high as an indefatigable, earnest, successful winner of souls, and as a burning and shining light that helped to fill the Principality with the radiance of the pure gospel.'

Thomas Raffles (1788–1863), the Independent minister of Great George Street Chapel, Liverpool, and himself a celebrated preacher, acknowledged Christmas Evans to be 'the mightiest preacher of the age'; the British prime minister, David Lloyd George, whose knowledge of Welsh preachers was quite extensive, said, 'One of the things that I should like to enjoy when I enter paradise is a preaching festival with John Elias, Christmas Evans, Williams of Wern and others occupying the pulpit. That is how these fathers of Nonconformity appeal to me.'

D. M. Lloyd-Jones, who needs no introduction to evangelical Christians, speaks of 'the great Christmas Evans, who, some would say, was the greatest preacher that the Baptists have ever had in Great Britain— certainly he and Spurgeon would be the two greatest'; and the *Freeman*, a widely read nineteenth-century English Baptist journal, after observing that 'the coming of Mr Spurgeon to any city, town or village, either in England, Wales or Scotland, is an event which moves the entire population, Church and Nonconforming, rich and poor, church-going and non church-going', summed up by remarking: 'No other preacher in this age wields such power, and it may be questioned whether anyone else has ever done it in these islands save John Knox in Scotland and Christmas Evans in Wales.'

I would like to express my thanks to Evangelical Press for allowing me to make this abridgement of my original work on Christmas Evans, published in 2001, and to Day One Publications for their willingness and enthusiasm to make the story of this great man and preacher available to a wider readership.

Glossary

Some of the words in the text may be unfamiliar to some readers. It is hoped that the brief definitions given will help them to understand more about the life of Christmas Evans.

Arianism

The term is derived from the name of Arius, a bishop of Alexandria, whose doctrine of the Trinity was condemned at the Council of Nicaea in AD325. He taught that God the Son was the first creature of the Father and there was a time when God the Son did not exist. It follows that the Son cannot be of the same nature as the Father. Jehovah's Witnesses are the modern-day Arians.

Arminianism

The term is derived from the name of James Harmens (in Latin: *Jacobus Arminius*) who became Professor of Divinity at Leyden University at the end of the sixteenth century. In 1591 he began to doubt the truths he had been taught at Geneva (where John Calvin taught). The principal difference between his teachings and those of Calvin was on the nature of predestination. Calvin taught that this was *absolute* and Arminius taught that it was *conditional*, that is, that believers can lose their salvation. This was the essential point of difference between the Wesleys and Whitefield.

Fullerism

The term is derived from the name of Andrew Fuller, who in the nineteenth century separated from other Calvinists because he felt that they were not evangelical in their preaching. The term 'hyper-Calvinism' was used to describe these non-evangelical Calvinists.

Sabellianism

The term is derived from the name of Sabellius, a presbyter of Ptolemais in AD250 (modern Akko in northern Israel), who, in his desire to maintain the absolute unity of God, denied that the distinctions (Father, Son and Holy Spirit) within the Godhead were ultimate or permanent. His teaching was condemned by the council of Rome in AD260, and he was excommunicated by Pope Calixtus.

Sandemanianism
This term is fully explained within the text at the appropriate point.

Socinianism
The term is derived from Faustus Socinus (in Italian: *Fausto Paulo Sozini*). He developed anti-Trinitarian views and became leader of the sect named after him. He was denounced as a heretic in 1590.

A troubled upbringing

Christmas Evans was born in a small cottage called Esgair Wen, located in the Dyffryn Llynod valley near the village of Tre-groes in the parish of Llandysul on 25 December 1766, during a stormy winter. The nearby village of Llandysul, lying on the banks of the River Teifi and set in the picturesque Cardiganshire hills, consisted of only a few homes in the middle of the eighteenth century. The surrounding district, with its wooded slopes and bleak pastoral uplands, was barely accessible to outsiders. The population of Wales was about 500,000 and 'its people were mostly small farmers and labourers, living in thinly-populated, isolated communities, with few towns or centres of population. Most of them were illiterate or barely literate, and too poor to be able to buy books.'

Christmas was the middle child of Samuel and Joanna Evans, who named him Christmas either after the day of his birth, or after Samuel's brother, who must also have been born on Christmas Day. At birth he was so frail and small that he could fit snugly into a quart container. His mother, because of his size, did not expect him to survive.

Nothing is known about his older sister and there is little information concerning his younger brother John, who grew up to be a 'solitary self-contained man, leading an objectless, semi-vagrant life, in the poorest circumstances, with little to comfort him except the reflected greatness of Christmas, of which he availed himself in his wanderings'. As adults he and Christmas looked very much alike. Both were tall, bony and not very good-looking, and both had only one eye, John having lost his in some accident or fight.

Samuel Evans and Joanna Lewis were married on 19 December 1761, in the parish of Llandysul. Joanna was illiterate and marked her name with a cross in the register. Samuel was a shoemaker from Llangeler who, for most of his life, fought against ill health. Joanna came from a respectable family of freeholders in the parish, who offered Christmas little financial assistance during his poor and troubled youth. However, he did not hold them accountable for his hardships, as in after years, when well-known

*Christmas Evans was born in a small cottage called Esgair Wen,
located in the Dyffryn Llynod valley near the village of Tre-groes*

The field where the cottage Esgair Wen was located

*Oak tree planted in 1938 in memory
of Christmas Evans's birthplace*

throughout the Principality, he visited them, preached in their houses and in return was treated by them with great respect.

Little is known about Joanna's character and faith (partly due to her son's reticence to speak of his family) except that she urged him, when a boy, to consider spiritual matters, especially his eternal welfare and destiny. One of his few references to her is in a sermon on *The Parable of the Prodigal Son*, in which he comments, 'I remember my godly mother saying to me, "Christmas, my boy, think of your soul;" and I would say jeeringly, "Do you hear how mother can preach?"' His parents were very poor and unable to offer him or his brother and sister any formal education.

During his childhood some remarkable deliverances from misfortunes and accidents occurred in which he saw the protecting hand of God. The first of these took place when he was eight years old. He went into the fields to plough on the back of a very wild horse, which suddenly bolted down a hill and towards the stable. Without slowing, it galloped through the stable

Notice attached to the oak tree

door with Christmas still clinging to its back. Amazingly, its terrified rider was not injured. Years later, when he examined and measured the stable door, he was unable to fathom how he had escaped without injury, remarking, 'It was through God's good providence that I was not struck dead at the entrance door.'

When aged nine he climbed up into a tree with the intention of cutting down a branch. He had his knife open in his hand, and was resting upon one branch and taking hold of another in order to cut it, when one of the branches broke, and he fell down from a great height. He remained there on the ground until the afternoon, when he was discovered in a state of unconsciousness. When he remembered this accident he wondered how he had not been killed, or at least why his bones had not been broken, concluding that God was keeping him for some special future work.

These incidents had a profound effect on him, alerting him to the perils and fragility of life, and, no doubt recalling his mother's exhortations, to the closeness of eternity. But it was another more devastating occurrence that was to change the course of his life. In 1775 his father died, leaving

Joanna destitute and wholly dependent on the support of the parish and any kind-hearted friends of the family, whose hearts were far larger than their fortunes.

From his father's funeral he dates his first religious impressions, when he was 'much terrified with the fear of death, and of the day of judgement', which caused him great anxiety, especially at night, and induced him 'to make some kinds of prayers'; yet 'these thoughts of terror were not of long continuance—they vanished, and recurred now and again'. Near the end of his life he said, 'I was disturbed by certain operations of mind, which, I believe, were not common, from my ninth year upwards. The fear of dying in an ungodly state especially affected me, and this apprehension clung to me till I was induced to rest upon Christ. All this was accompanied by some little knowledge of the Redeemer; and now, in my seventieth year, I cannot deny that this concern was the dawn of the day of grace on my spirit, although mingled with much darkness and ignorance.'

Joanna Evans, bound by the straits of poverty, struggled to bring up her children on her own. Before long, to relieve the pressures at home and with the intention of securing a more prosperous future for Christmas, who had already been helping with the family finances for over a year, she sent him to her brother James Lewis, who owned a farm at Bwlchog in the nearby parish of Llanfihangel-ar-arth. Uncle Lewis was a 'cruel, selfish and drunken man', who, in spite of his promise to feed and clothe Christmas in return for his labours on the farm, treated his nephew with contempt, working him ruthlessly. He refused him any schooling, and gave him no moral or religious instruction, so that when he left four years later he could not read a single word, knew nothing of books or the Bible, and had spent the formative years of his life witnessing the drunkenness of a family member.

It was while working at Ty-newydd Farm in Llanfihangel-ar-arth that he experienced another remarkable escape. He was about twelve years old and walking in a field through which a rapid river flowed and in which there had just been a great flood. He drew near to inspect a deep whirlpool, which the flood had formed. Suddenly the ground gave way beneath him and he was thrown into the water. There was no one nearby and no branch or post onto which he could cling. Somehow, after a great struggle, he

Ty-newydd Farm in Llanfihangel-ar-arth where Christmas Evans worked for his Uncle Lewis

managed to scramble out. He could never say how his life was saved, as it had seemed impossible for him to pull himself out of the swirling waters.

During these miserable years working for his uncle mainly as a shepherd, 'he was not wanted anywhere. He lived among the beasts of the field by night as well as by day, for no human desired his company.' Understandably, all his recollections of his youth, and particularly of James Lewis, were painfully bitter. In later life he said of his uncle, 'It would be difficult to find a more unconscionable man than James Lewis in the whole course of a wicked world.' When he finally left Bwlchog, he was a poor, homeless, friendless teenager, whose 'very condition in life condemned him into association with whatever was rude, unreflecting and brutal in his neighbourhood', and whose prospects for usefulness appeared pitifully poor.

Converted

After Bwlchog, Christmas worked for several farmers successively in his native parish of Llandysul. At Pen-yr-allt Fawr his standard of living improved slightly, and at Glanclettwr near Pont-siân he was shown kindness and respect, though food supplies were meagre. At Glanclettwr, when he was about fifteen, he was one day out on the mountain watching the sheep, when 'a dispute arose between him and another shepherd; and in the contention, this other shepherd drew out his knife and stabbed him in the right breast; the knife, however, touched a bone and glanced off without inflicting any mortal injury'.

He also worked at Castell Hywel on a farm that was owned by the Arian minister David Davis (1745–1827), who was to exercise such a deep influence on him. At this period he was still illiterate and described as 'remarkable even among his fellows for uncouthness and rusticity, and bore about him an awkward, ponderous individuality, which might, according to circumstances, develop into some sort of notoriety or distinction—a large-boned, muscular, much-brooding and somewhat passionate young man'. He was given to frequent meditations, and possessed a lively imagination, although there was no hint of the genius that would soon captivate Wales.

In 1783, when Christmas Evans was sixteen and perhaps an occasional churchgoer, a religious revival occurred in the Arminian Presbyterian Church at Llwynrhydowen, the first Arminian church in Wales. At the time of Christmas Evans the church was almost Unitarian in its beliefs. Its pastor, David Davis, a generous and benevolent man from the Carmarthen Presbyterian College, was noted, among other things, for his prodigious size.

In 1782, Davis founded the Academy at Castell Hywel, which thrived for thirty years. He educated many of the clergy and Dissenting ministers of that part of Wales, especially those who could not afford to study at university, and boys from all over the locality came to study in his school. However, he had very indefinite views on Christian doctrine, and leaned towards Arianism.

Llwynrhydowen, the first Arminian church in Wales

Castell Hywel School, where Christmas Evans was taught for six months

Plaque on a wall at Castell Hywel

He was particularly accommodating to the youth in the church, allowing them scope and freedom in discussion, and encouraging them to discover the truth for themselves. He can rightly be called Christmas Evans's first instructor, philosopher and friend.

The revival of religion at Llwynrhydowen, which Christmas Evans soon heard about and participated in, spread throughout the church and many in the congregation, particularly among the young, turned to Christ. 'Religion became the only thing that mattered. Services at the chapel and elsewhere were continued for endless hours during the day and night. When the ecstasy began to wane among the older folk it was rekindled among the young. The second flame of fire was more captivatingly furious and thorough than the first, and many who had not felt the first in its heat and warmth came into contact with the second and were caught by it. Its warmth changed them.'

During the revival a great change for good came over Christmas Evans. He became serious in manner and outlook, prayed much, vowed to lead a better life, and, along with the other converts, joined the church. However,

Plaque in Tre-groes on a school wall

his early 'Christian experience was evidently very imperfect. He had a conviction of the evil of sin, and a desire to flee from the wrath to come, but no evidence of acceptance with God, and a very limited knowledge of the plan of salvation. Yet his religious impressions were not entirely fruitless. They produced, at least, a partial reformation of life, and led to many penitential resolutions. He thought much of eternity, and was often in secret prayer.'

After this spiritual awakening he realised more and more that the Christian must have 'a rock in the merits of the Redeemer to rest upon', and that that rock is a 'place of refuge and a covert from the storm and the rain'. In an ever-increasing measure 'the spirit of energetic supplication' was poured out on him, although, according to his own testimony, such a spirit was accompanied by fear and ignorance.

As has been mentioned, he had at this time a confused knowledge of the way of salvation and a rather shallow experience of it in his heart, but he earnestly desired to read the Bible, which he accomplished with very little aid. He also studied other branches of learning in order to try to make up what was lacking in his education.

His pastor, David Davis, who was very keen to promote the intellectual standing of his congregation and who noticed his desire to progress in this area, took a keen interest in him and invited him to his school, which was the only formal education he ever received. His learned teacher maintained that he never had a young man who made so much progress in so short a time, and under such disadvantageous circumstances. He soon became a popular pupil with the whole Davis family. 'He was a very sober man,' said David Davis's second son Timothy, 'always with us during our prayer meetings. I remember him carrying me in his arms to the chapel at Llwynrhydowen.'

Recollecting this time much later in life, Christmas Evans says: 'One of the fruits of this awakening was the desire for religious knowledge that fell upon us. Scarcely one person out of ten could, at this time, and in those neighbourhoods, read at all, even in the language of the country. We bought Bibles and candles, and were accustomed to meet together in the evening, in the barn of Penyralltfawr; and thus, in about one month, I was able to read the Bible in my mother tongue. I was vastly delighted with so much learning. This, however, did not satisfy me, but I borrowed books and learnt a little English. Mr Davis, my pastor, understood that I thirsted for knowledge, and he took me to his school, where I stayed for six months.'

There is an interesting story connected with Christmas Evans's entry to his pastor's school. One evening he asked the senior farm hand, John, if he could go to church the following Sunday to hear David Davis preach. John agreed and promised to take care of the farm animals while he was away. On the Sabbath morning he arrived at the church in a serious mood, and throughout the whole service sat with his head in his hands and his elbows resting on his knees. As soon as the service was over, without saying a word, he hurried home.

David Davis had noticed the young man's strange behaviour and after dinner sent for John to see if he could explain it. John asked his pastor to follow him and together they crept into a field to find Christmas standing before a congregation of cows, horses and sheep! He had erected a shelter of branches near the hedge for his protection and fashioned a pulpit out of twigs. As they approached they witnessed him commence a 'mock' service that was almost identical to the morning service in the church: he announced a hymn and sang it; he read the Scriptures and then preached, practically word for word, David Davis's sermon; afterwards he prayed and sang a concluding hymn, during which the two humans in the congregation quietly escaped from the hallowed ground.

On the way home Davis asked John if he knew of another young man who could replace Christmas on the farm so he could take the budding preacher into his school. That evening John told Christmas he was no longer needed on the farm and that Davis wanted to speak with him. Christmas, fearing the worst, thought he was about to be dismissed for some misdemeanour and began to weep, but his anxieties were soon dispelled when he heard his pastor say, 'You are to come to my school to be educated free of charge.'

Starting to preach

The early Christian experiences of Christmas Evans were soon followed by a desire to preach the gospel. After joining the church at Llwynrhydowen he was called on to pray in public and in the various prayer meetings. Noticing his gifts, some of the congregation asked him to say a few words to them by way of exhortation. 'To this,' he says, 'I felt a strong inclination, though I was, as it were, a heap of spiritual ignorance.'

His first performance was well received so he was inclined to continue. His first full sermon was preached at Tybedw, Pentre-cwrt, in a cottage belonging to a kind tailor, David Hughes, who gave singing lessons in the neighbourhood and who helped the young men to read. According to his own confession, this sermon, preached 'at a prayer meeting which was held in a house in the parish of Llangeler', Carmarthenshire, was not original, but taken from a book he had probably borrowed from his pastor.

He also owns up to another instance of plagiarism: 'My first sermon was a translation of one of Bishop Beveridge's from *Thesaurus Theologicus*. One of my hearers said, "Had Mr D. Davis heard it, he would be ashamed to preach himself." But I had no faith in myself—I knew my poverty.

'I remember, too, securing a copy of the seven published sermons of Mr Rowland of Llangeitho. In later years I learned that he also had borrowed them. I memorised one of these sermons and preached it near Llwynrhydowen, where Mr Davies of Gamnant was listening. He was surprised to hear such a mighty sermon from such a young preacher. But within a week the praises vanished like Jonah's gourd, for Mr Davies had secured a copy of the volume that contained the seven sermons. "But," said he, "I believe there is something great in the son of Samuel the shoemaker, for his prayer was equal to his sermon." But that was no praise to me, for I knew that the prayer was memorised word for word from the prayer book of the Rev. Griffith Jones of Llanddowror. I had begun before I had gathered knowledge, and before *the vessels were opened*, as it were, to receive information.'

After his first sermon he received a few invitations to preach in the neighbourhood, but found it very hard to earn enough money to support himself. At most of the chapels he visited he was given the nominal fee of one shilling, which meant that, in spite of his pastor's generosity, he could only stay in school for six months.

To relieve these financial straits he journeyed in the autumn of 1784 or 1785 to Herefordshire to work during the harvest, a common enough venture for Welsh agricultural labourers who wanted to supplement their purses. Probably his original intention was to earn enough money to return to school. However, while he was in England he fell into a state of spiritual indifference and, tempted to pursue a secular employment, contemplated leaving school and turning his back on the ministry. School, to his mind, was unaffordable, and the ministry offered only a life of hardships and toil.

While considering the matter he was set upon one night by a group of ruffians—an attack he interpreted as a divine chastisement: 'I thought of relinquishing the work of the ministry, and the school altogether, and of engaging again in secular pursuits; but for this I was sharply reproved. A man, in connection with four or five others, agreed to waylay, overpower and stone me to death; one of them struck me on my right eye with a cudgel, so that I lost it on the spot. I was also violently beaten on the head, which utterly deprived me of my senses, and I lay for some time as dead.'

His one eye was often the focus of attention, provoking comments from all sorts of people. Once when someone was making fun of Welsh preachers before Robert Hall, an eloquent English Baptist preacher and a shrewd apologist for Christianity, upon mentioning Christmas Evans, the jester said, 'And he only has one eye!' 'Yes, sir,' answered Robert Hall, 'but that's a piercer; an eye, sir, that could light an army through a wilderness in a dark night.' On another occasion the same preacher described his contemporary as 'the tallest, the stoutest and the greatest man I ever saw; that he had but one eye, if it could be called an eye; it was more properly a brilliant star—it shone like Venus!'

The night he lost his eye he 'saw in a dream, that the day of judgement was come, and I beheld Jesus on the clouds and all the world on fire; and I was in great fear, yet crying earnestly, and with some confidence, for his peace. He answered and said, "Thou thoughtest to be a preacher, but what wilt thou do now? The world is on fire and it is too late!" This restored me from my backsliding, and I felt heartily thankful when I awoke that I was in bed.' This dream left a deep impression on his mind, as did many dreams throughout his career, and he remembered it for a considerable time. In later years he reasoned that some of the most important intimations of his life had been given to him through dreams, 'and it was utterly vain to attempt to persuade him to the contrary'.

He determined to return to God and to the calling that was upon his life. He started to read the Bible regularly and to observe seasons of prayer, much to the annoyance of his fellow haymakers, who beat him in order to drive religion from him; but their cruelty served only to strengthen his resolve to continue in the ministry. He returned to Wales and began to preach with new energy and success. Those who heard him delighted in what he said and encouraged him to continue. His friends predicted that he would yet 'become a great man, and a celebrated preacher'.

Baptised

Christmas received considerable encouragement at this stage from William Perkins, an Independent minister at Pantycreuddyn and Pencader, who frequently opened his pulpit to the young preacher, offered him friendship and understanding, and even placed his library at his disposal. Perkins was an 'able, eloquent and popular preacher, but addicted to intemperance. His churches failed to induce him to mend his ways, and majority decisions inhibited him from his ministry.'

There is a tradition connecting Perkins and Christmas Evans: 'About this time Perkins, having engaged to preach at a certain funeral, failed to fulfil his appointment; a prayer-meeting was therefore about to be held; whereupon a person present suggested that "the lad Christmas, Samuel the shoemaker's son", was in the cottage, who had, to his knowledge, a stock of sermons in hand, and would preach as well as Mr Perkins himself. "The lad Christmas", then eighteen or nineteen years old, undertook to preach at this short notice, and went through the service to the satisfaction of his audience.'

One of the churches Christmas visited every month was a branch of Llwynrhydowen at Mydroilyn about ten miles north of Llandysul. He was also well received by the small congregation at Crug-y-maen and at Pantycreuddyn. The pulpits of the Methodists of Cefn Llanfair and the Baptists at Pen-y-bont, Llandysul, where he preached on many occasions, were also open to him. Of the latter congregation he speaks very highly, noting that there were men and women 'who were eminent for their experimental knowledge of the grace of God', and whose conversations were 'a blessing to me'.

Unfortunately, at least as far as Welsh Presbyterianism is concerned, there was a law in the church stating that no member would be permitted to preach without first passing through a college course, an impossible demand for Christmas Evans as he was extremely poor and without the assistance of influential friends. Consequently he left the church in order to preach the gospel, joining the Baptists.

Although his early ministry was blessed of God and the responses of those who heard him were favourable, Christmas Evans lacked confidence

Baptist Church at Aberduar

in preaching and, for the next three years, was somewhat confused about his beliefs. He had little peace with God and was often tormented by feelings of guilt and inadequacy. He doubted his own salvation and became more and more dissatisfied with the life of the church and his pastor's preaching, which tended to induce self-righteousness, thereby contradicting his own experience and further exasperating his muddled state of mind. His heart, to use his own expression, was 'a *little hell* within him'. Yet, as he records, he was gratefully preserved from Arminianism and Socinianism, doctrines that were upheld by several men of exceptional talent at that time and which prevailed fairly extensively in what was called the most 'rationalistic' part of Wales.

He had obvious affection for his pastor, but he could not help noticing that many of the other preachers he heard had distinct and more biblical views of the gospel than David Davis, and that the worship at Llwynrhydowen was formal and cold, unlike the warm and fervent worship of the Baptist Church at Aberduar, which he occasionally visited. He found himself increasingly attracted to Christians who held Calvinist doctrines and was impressed by their godliness and knowledge of the Word. As he studied the Bible for himself, he realised that the Calvinistic Baptists were much nearer the truth than the Arminians with whom he worshipped.

It was during this period of uncertainty that he became unsettled about baptism, a doctrine he had not seriously considered before. He says, 'I had always regarded the Baptists as Anabaptists, as *re*-baptizing, and from my infancy had always heard them called Anabaptists; nor had I ever understood that any man of my condition had searched the Bible for himself, to ascertain what baptism it enjoined.' Evan Amos,

Pen-y-bont Baptist Church at Llandysul, where Christmas Evans often preached

who had left Llwynrhydowen for the Calvinistic Baptist Church at Aberduar, where he had been baptised by Timothy Thomas, challenged him on the matter and eventually he was convinced about 'the necessity of obeying the baptism instituted by Christ'.

'This man paid me a visit one day, when I attacked him with some severity upon the errors of the Anabaptists, but Amos silenced me very soon. I thought that his vanquishing me so easily was owing to my ignorance and unacquaintedness with the New Testament. I commenced reading, beginning in Matthew, in order to prepare myself with a sufficient number of Scriptures to meet Amos at the next interview. After having gone through the whole of the New Testament, I could not find one passage substantiating the rite of infant baptism. I frequently met with passages in the Old Testament, and some in the New, referring to the circumcision of children, to the naming of children, and to the training of

New Pen-y-bont Baptist Church at Llandysul

children up in the nurture and admonition of the Lord; but not one for the baptising of children. I found about forty passages that gave their testimony in the plainest and most unhesitating manner for baptising on a profession of faith. They spoke of conscience, and convinced me of the necessity of obeying the baptism instituted by Christ, who required me to yield personal obedience to him.

'After a little struggling between flesh and spirit, between obedience and disobedience, I went to the Baptist Church at Aberduar, in the parish of Llanybyther, in the county of Carmarthen. I was cordially received there, but not without a degree of dread on the part of some, that I was still a stout-hearted Arminian.'

Friends suggested to him that he ought to be baptised and furnished him with relevant books on the subject. After a strict examination before the church, he was baptised, with nine others, by Timothy Thomas, one of his new pastors, in the River Duar in the summer of 1788 and admitted to the communion of the church. He was twenty-one years old.

Depressed

Although Daniel Rowland and Howel Harris were converted in 1735, the evangelical awakening in Wales did not really influence Baptist and Independent congregations until the mid-1770s. At the time Christmas Evans joined the Baptists, the denomination was about to enjoy its second period of growth and spiritual renewal. One of the churches to share in this revival was Aberduar, where 'scores were awakened to a sense of the state of their souls, a great degree of religious rejoicing was experienced, and the sound of praise was heard through the whole neighbourhood'.

These new converts were filled with an 'inexpressible and glorious joy' that manifested itself in ecstatic bodily movements, arm-wavings, and enthusiastic singing and laughing, called 'Welsh Jumping' by those who disapproved. At first, notes Christmas Evans, 'such life and animation in divine worship greatly surprised me, for I knew nothing of religious enjoyment heretofore. I had experienced some taste of it whilst preaching on one occasion [at Cefn Llanfair], with one of the Calvinistic Methodists, and the relish of it remained with me asleep and awake for some days; but now, among my new friends, I could not help viewing myself as a speckled bird, not feeling what they felt, until my mind was filled with very low and dejected thoughts of my state and condition.' It was about a year later, after he had studied much and been fervent in prayer, that he experienced an inner release of the Spirit.

His new pastor, Timothy Thomas 'II' (1754–1840), was a man of strong and clear faith and whose fervent preaching had a profound influence on many, including Christmas Evans. Thomas welcomed Christmas Evans into the Baptist Church and, with patience and power, helped him to become more settled in his beliefs and more forthright in his preaching. In his later life, when asked how many he had baptised, he would answer abruptly, 'About two thousand!' Sometimes he replied: 'I have baptised at least two thousand persons. Yes, thirty of them have become ministers of the gospel; and it was I who baptised Christmas Evans.'

With godly influences around him, and experiencing a new environment of enthusiasm and zeal for the things of God, Christmas Evans received much spiritual good, and was greatly helped to embrace, albeit slowly, the Calvinistic doctrines and to form more definite views of the person of Christ. 'He himself observes, that joining the Baptists was of great benefit to him—bringing him to behold the righteousness of Christ imputed to him that believeth, and the blood of Jesus Christ "purifying the conscience from dead works to serve the living God"—and also, that hearing some of the most eminent ministers of the day, of different denominations, was greatly blessed, to lead him to consider the doctrine of the grace of God through a Mediator, without any human merit.'

There is little doubt that Christmas Evans was aroused and inspired by these fine men and fed 'manna from heaven', but they had another salutary effect on him. He started to compare himself with them, and with other preachers of his new denomination, and found them 'altogether better and godlier preachers than I was'. 'I entertained,' he said, 'the highest thoughts of every other preacher, but none of myself. I conceived that every person who was born again, and had believed, was endowed with much better light in divine things than I possessed.'

This led him to entertain depressing views of his own Christian character and ministry. He imagined he was not endowed with the necessary gifts for ministry, despaired every time he heard his own voice, and, conscious of his appearance, entered the pulpit with dread, thinking that the mere sight of him was enough to cast a gloom over the service and cloud his hearers' minds. When he looked back over the years he had been preaching, he could not ascertain that he had been the means of salvation to a single soul. These feelings of inadequacy caused him such overwhelming distress that he sometimes rolled himself on the floor in the deepest agony of mind.

This experience and the adoption of a different method of preaching he himself describes: 'I could feel no influence, no virtue in my own sermons. It occurred to me that this might be owing to my habit of committing my sermons carefully to memory, and that I thus superseded the Divine aid, while I supposed other preachers had theirs direct from heaven. I accordingly changed my plan, and would take a text and preach from it without preparation, saying whatever would come uppermost at the time;

but if it was bad before, it now was still worse, for I had neither sense, nor warmth, nor life; but some weakly intonation of voice that affected no one. It was painful to me to hear my own voice in prayer or in preaching, as it seemed to proceed from a hard heart.

'I travelled much in this condition, thinking every preacher a true preacher but myself; nor had I any confidence in the light I had upon Scripture. I considered everybody to be before myself, and was frequently tortured with fears that I was still a graceless man. I have since seen God's goodness in all this, for thus was I kept from falling in love with my own gifts, which has happened to many young men, and has been their ruin.'

To make matters worse he had 'no friend under the sun, to whom I could open my mind, and disclose the plague of my heart; I dared not unbosom myself, for I thought if any knew how it was with me, they would at once conclude that I was an unconverted man, and expose me to the whole world.' Though he entertained such depressing views of himself and was unconscious of the power of God on his ministry, all who knew him thought him to be an excellent Christian and had full confidence in his piety.

These battles with depression, recurring as they did throughout his life, were aids to prepare him for usefulness as a pastor and preacher, and to keep his spirit in humble dependence on God in the midst of great success.

Chapter 6

Transformed

At this stage in his career, Christmas Evans had no idea that he was about to depart for North Wales, where he would labour so effectively for over forty years. His ministry in that part of the Principality, as we shall see, was singularly blessed of God, producing a lasting impact on the Baptist denomination there and, with the help of his contemporaries, on society as a whole. Coupled with his yearly tours to the South, his success in the North made him one of the most popular and powerful preachers of all time.

On 9–10 June 1789, after the harvest, the Baptist churches of South and West Wales assembled at Maes-y-berllan chapel in Brecknockshire for an Association meeting, and 'The chief matter under discussion on the practical and administrative side was the evangelisation of North Wales. Reports of the work already accomplished were presented, but they all agreed that a settled ministry was the great need of the land.' Christmas Evans walked all the way from Aberduar and arrived on the Tuesday afternoon at Maes-y-berllan, prepared to read the churches' letters and in the hope of being sent north to preach the gospel, a hope he had before occasionally entertained. This was the first Association meeting he attended.

During the meeting Christmas Evans met several preachers from North Wales, who explained to him the field of labour open in the North and the great shortage of gospel preachers and, on the recommendation of his pastor Timothy Thomas and of others who had heard glowing reports about his preaching, they urged him to return with them.

With much trepidation, but without a thought of returning home to bid farewell to his friends, he consented to accompany them, going through Merionethshire, where J. R. Jones left the party, and then into Caernarfonshire, where he preached in Criccieth with Williams of Cheltenham. He arrived at the extreme corner of the country called Lleyn in July 1789. All was not well, though, for in spite of a pleasant journey, with opportunities of preaching in the different churches along the way, 'the heavy burden that lay on his mind, like the burden of Bunyan's pilgrim, continued to oppress him'.

Site of the first Baptist Chapel in Nefyn

'This is the site of the first Baptist Chapel in Nefyn: built 1785, rebuilt 1850, demolished 1926'

Old graveyard attached to the first Baptist Chapel in Nefyn

Plaque on the top of Ty'ndonen Chapel

Lleyn, in the north-western part of Wales, is a wild, remote but beautiful tract of country, about twenty-five miles long and from five to ten miles broad, and surrounded by impressive hills and overhanging mountains. The Baptist cause in Lleyn, formed about five years before Christmas Evans's arrival, was feeble and disorganised. The mother church was Salem Ty'ndonen in the parish of Botwnnog, with branches at Llangïan, Rhoshirwaun, Galltraeth and Nefyn. There had been no minister at these places since David Morris left in 1785 for the church at Porth Tywyll in Carmarthen, and their small congregations were eager to receive the new preacher from the South.

The mother church of the Baptist cause in Lleyn was Salem, Ty'ndonnen in the parish of Botwnnog

At each of the stations there was a place of worship and every Sunday, in an effort to preach throughout the peninsula, Christmas Evans travelled on foot from one to another. In the week he preached at midday or in the afternoon, as well as in the evening, so long as there was a congregation, large or small, ready to listen. He had few books to aid his preparations: the Bible, a borrowed Welsh–English dictionary, a Welsh translation of Bunyan's *Pilgrim's Progress*; and William Burkitt on the New Testament, which he would study in bed at night, looking up the more difficult words in his dictionary, and which became so important to him that the residents renamed it Christmas Evans's *Barcud*.

Within a month of his arrival he was ordained at Salem Ty'ndonen as missionary preacher to itinerate among the small churches. The public service was traditional, with the two officiating ministers, John Evans and

Christmas Evans was ordained at Ty'ndonen in 1789

Thomas Morris, at the time the only available ministers in the neighbourhood, laying on hands. Such an appointment was regarded by the few Baptists in the area as highly significant and indicative of God's blessing towards them.

From the beginning of his ministry in Lleyn he was invigorated and inspired, and brought into the light and liberty of the gospel. It was as if a new day had dawned on his personal religion. His confidence in prayer grew and he experienced a deeper sense of rest and peace in Christ. He started to enjoy the Christian life, to judge religious matters for himself, instead of relying too heavily on the opinions of others, and to understand more fully his calling to preach Christ, although the old doubts continued to surface every so often. Through the study of the Scriptures, 'the last vestiges of Arminianism disappeared from his theology' to be replaced by the Calvinistic doctrines of grace.

A new power attended his preaching, which was to rest on him for the whole of his life, though it was obscured for a time during his involvement with Sandemanianism. He was vibrant and full of passion in the pulpit, with a strength and conviction in his ministry, overflowing with love, and anxious for the salvation of souls. His congregations, said one of his converts, Evan Evans of Llanarmon, would 'weep, cry out and jump up and down as though the world was bursting into flames around them' and a revival of religious feeling awoke wherever he went. 'A breeze from the New Jerusalem,' he wrote many years later, 'descended upon me and on the people, and many were awakened to eternal life.'

In a relatively short time the religious life of the district was changed from a cold deadness to life and power in Christ. He himself was surprised by the fruit of his labour, especially when those who came before the church as candidates for membership attributed their conversion to his ministry, 'because,' as he observes, 'I had been for three years preaching, and never had received any intimation that one sinner had been converted, and also on account of the old feelings of despondency and fear which yet occasionally troubled me; still I was obliged to believe, and it was wondrous in my eyes.' His own ministry there, so he thought, was owned of God to as great an extent as any other place in which he subsequently laboured, perhaps with the exception of Caerphilly.

It was while at Lleyn that he had frequent opportunities of hearing several godly men, whose manner and spirit of preaching deeply affected his own ministry and prepared him, as a servant of God, for greater and more universal usefulness.

The man who most influenced Christmas Evans during his Lleyn ministry, especially by his style of preaching, was Robert Roberts (1762–1802), 'one of the brightest stars of the Welsh pulpit'. He was an extraordinary preacher, with extraordinary powers of oratory, and remarkable for the authority and effects that attended his ministry. It is said that he was capable of riveting the attention of his hearers simply by reading his text. He possessed great physical energy, a beautiful and penetrating voice, a fine memory, and a keen grasp of the truth, all of which were combined with wonderful dramatic and imaginative powers.

It was the dramatic effect of Roberts's sermons, coupled with his bold and original imagination, that moved Christmas Evans to adopt a new style of preaching. Once, when he heard Roberts in a certain place, 'where he drew one of his graphic pictures, and made a bright light to play upon it, until the eyes of all the people were riveted in attention', he exclaimed after the sermon, 'I also could preach in that manner, but I never ventured; I shall try from henceforth.' He did try, and as a 'natural consequence of this change in tone and manner of his preaching, [even] great[er] success followed his efforts'.

During his time in Lleyn he lost no opportunity of hearing Roberts, and in subsequent years, when asked about his own unusual way of preaching, he was always ready to explain: 'I had the ideas before, but somehow couldn't get at them. When I was in Lleyn, the Methodists had a preacher of the name Robert Roberts of Llanllyfni, who was very popular, and there was a great deal of talk about him. Well, I went on one Sunday afternoon [to Rhydyclafdy] to hear him. He was one of the most insignificant-looking persons I ever saw—a little hunchbacked man; but he neither thought nor said anything like other people; there was something wonderful and uncommon about him. This Robert Roberts gave me the key.'

Tyn-y-mur farm, where Christmas Evans probably preached before a Baptist Chapel was built next door

First preaching tour

It was during the first year of his ministry on the Lleyn peninsula, which he often referred to as the most important of his life, that he met and fell in love with Catherine Jones, a poor and illiterate member of the same church. Catherine was born at Pwllheli in 1766 and converted when she was about nineteen. From the time of her conversion she experienced a deep sense of her own corruption, saw the 'indispensable necessity' of the merits of Christ for salvation, and realised the need for the renovating influence of the Holy Spirit in her life.

She joined the Baptist church at Lleyn and was baptised by Daniel Davies of Llanelli, Carmarthenshire. She married Christmas in the church at Bryncroes on 23 October 1789, in the twenty-third year of their ages, and the people of the area gave them £15 as a wedding present. Christmas, in a tribute he wrote after her death, comments, 'In her the designation *help-meet* was signally verified. Her husband must long remember her affectionate kindness in straits and difficulty.'

Catherine Evans proved a faithful and compatible soul mate, prepared to endure every hardship occasioned by her devotion to Christ and to her husband. She was kind, thoughtful and generous in her dealings with others, in spite of subsisting on meagre rations of oatmeal, buttermilk and potatoes. 'It is almost incredible,' says Christmas in his tribute, 'that she should have been so extensively charitable, when her husband's income never surpassed *thirty* pounds a year. What food she gave away to poor children and needy folks! Garments to poor members of the church! Money and bread to thousands of Irish labourers, who passed her door on their way to and from the English harvests! Her house was always open to itinerant ministers, and she readily administered to them with her own hands.'

Once Christmas responded playfully to her promptings to tend the garden by saying, 'Catherine fach, you never mind the potatoes; put your trust in Providence and all will be well.' She calmly replied, exhibiting her strong common sense, 'I tell you what we'll do, Christmas. You go and sit down on top of Moel y Gest, waiting for Providence, and I'll go and hoe the potatoes; and we shall see to which of us Providence will come first.' Needless to say, after such a gentle rebuke, he hurried to perform his duty.

After his marriage the ministerial responsibilities of the churches increased markedly. These extended over a large area and kept him from home night after night. He often preached five times on the Sabbath. The Baptist cause in those parts, hitherto very weak, was greatly strengthened by his constant labours, which were rewarded with so little remuneration that he could barely exist.

During his first year he baptised fifty people of all ages, but mostly poor, at Ty'ndonen, and eighty sought church membership the second year, though many of these actually joined the Calvinistic Methodists and some the Independents. Many years after he had left Lleyn one of the stewards of the Calvinistic Methodists there, testifying to the lasting change for good wrought in the lives of many through his ministry, told him at Nant, 'Your spiritual children are with us in great numbers in our societies unto this day.' Eventually the strain of the work told and in the second year of his settlement in Lleyn he suffered exhaustion and ill health. His friends feared consumption, but he was spared.

Surprisingly, in this weakened condition, he embarked in 1791 on a long preaching tour to South Wales, hoping the journey and a different sphere of labour among old friends would benefit his health. He could not procure a horse for the journey, as the societies he served were very poor, so he set out on foot, preaching at least once a day, often twice and occasionally three times, in every town and village through which he passed. Though he preached acceptably at these stations, there is no report of any extraordinary effects accompanying his ministry until he reached South Wales.

While he was heading for Beddgelert, probably on his first journey to South Wales, and somewhere between Pont Aberglaslyn and Maentwrog, the following incident occurred. He was greatly pained in his mind by the thought that he had not been called by heaven to the great work of the ministry. He was going on thus when this anxious fear pressed upon him heavier and heavier, so that, at last, he retired into the field to pray and to wrestle with God. After the struggle was over he felt himself a new man.

Great peace and consolation took possession of his mind ... he preached with great delight and with new power.'

Some years later Christmas Evans looked back and said: 'Although I had the gift of speaking, and was thirsting for knowledge that I might be able to teach others, and multitudes were eager to hear me, my fears pressed so heavily upon me that I dismounted, fastened my horse, and went into a field close by, which I will just now point out to you; for as I draw near the place I recollect it more vividly. Whether anyone saw me I heeded not, because the end of all things, as it were, had come upon me. However, God had mercy on my poor soul, and I received Jacob's blessing, dear brother; yes, I saw, as it were, the heavens open.

'When I arose, I started on my journey, and the smiles of the Heavenly Spirit lighted up my way for the space of two months. I have since that occasionally had my doubts and fears; but the fear I had not been called to the ministry never afterwards so troubled me. I have not the slightest doubt but that it is my duty to put forth all my power in the ministry as long as I live.'

During the tour he visited Aberystwyth, Newcastle Emlyn, Cardigan, Penyparc and Blaen-waun, as well as Newport, Fishguard and Tabor in Pembrokeshire. Many had never heard of him, yet they were amazed at the power and authority of his message, and the doctrines he preached with such rousing and stirring effect. Old acquaintances regarded him as a new man, and stood dumbfounded as a great awakening followed wherever he went, especially in the neighbourhood of Cardigan, where the churches enjoyed larger congregations for a year afterwards. If it was announced he was preaching, thousands would gather, filling chapels and graveyards, with many following him from one service to another for many miles.

Scores were converted, and the power of the preached Word and the effect it had on the crowds was extraordinary, as he himself describes: 'I now felt a power in the word, like a hammer breaking the rock, and not like a brush. The work of conversion was progressing so rapidly and with so much energy in those parts that the ordinance of baptism was administered every month for a year or more, at Cilfowyr, Cardigan, Blaen-waun, Blaen-y-ffos, and Ebenezer, to from ten to twenty persons each month. The chapels and adjoining burying grounds were crowded with hearers of a weekday, even in the middle of harvest. I frequently preached in the open air in the evenings, and the rejoicing, singing, and praising would continue until broad light the next morning. The hearers appeared melted down in tenderness at the different meetings, so that they wept streams of tears, and cried out in such a manner that one might suppose the whole congregation, male and female, was thoroughly dissolved by the gospel.

'Preaching was now unto me a pleasure, and the success of the ministry in all places was very great. The same people attended fifteen or twenty different meetings, many miles apart in the counties of Cardigan, Pembroke, Carmarthen, Glamorgan, Monmouth, and Brecknock. This revival, especially in the vicinity of Cardigan, and in Pembrokeshire, subdued the whole country, and induced people everywhere to think well of religion. The same heavenly gale followed down to Fishguard, Llangloffan, Little Newcastle, and Rhydwilym. There was such a tender spirit resting on the hearers at this season, from Tabor to Middlemill, that one would imagine, by their weeping and trembling in their places of worship, and all this mingled with so much heavenly cheerfulness, that they would wish to abide for ever in this state of mind.'

As he had originally hoped, the tour to South Wales revitalised his soul and invigorated his body. With the effects for good that accompanied his preaching and partly because these tours became an annual event, it did not take long for his fame to spread throughout the Principality, and in a short time he acquired a greater popularity in Wales than any other minister of his day.

He returned to Lleyn with great strength and confidence in God, yet the work among the Baptists there did not progress as quickly or as smoothly as he had hoped. Many who were blessed under his ministry decided not to join the Baptists, preferring to attach themselves to the flourishing, older and more established Calvinistic Methodist chapels, which discouraged their 'spiritual father' considerably. Thus, prompted by the leading of God, he began to search for a wider and more prosperous field of labour.

So after two years in Lleyn he moved to Anglesey. Looking back to his time in Caernarfonshire, he acknowledged, with a deep sense of gratitude to God, the development of his own ministry in that place and the many sinners who were converted under his preaching: 'The form and taste of my ministry has never been changed since I left Lleyn, despite all the revolutions I have passed through. I highly prize the recollections now, in my sixty-third year. It is probable I never had the favour of being the instrument to convert so many sinners, during the same period of time, until 1829, at Caerphilly.'

Anglesey

During the problems at Lleyn, Christmas Evans had looked for another field of labour, and, as he admits, 'prayed that God would send me to Anglesey in particular'. He also received what he calls a 'providential intimation' that he should move to the island and serve the Baptist Church there, when a farmer by the name of John Jones, coincidentally a Baptist deacon at Llangefni, invited him and his wife to the island. As expected, he did not hesitate to go with him. He commenced the journey on horseback, with his wife sitting behind him and their few personal belongings hanging from the side of the animal, on his twenty-fifth birthday, Christmas Day 1791.

According to his own account 'the way was long and the wind was cold; it was a very rough day of frost and snow'. Some time later he humorously referred to this journey as similar to attacking the North Pole! With the Caernarfonshire mountains and Snowdon on the right, watching over him all the way, and the sea and the Menai Strait ebbing and flowing on the left, he boarded the ferry to Anglesey and arrived, 'by the good hand of God', in the evening of the same day, tired and worn, at Llangefni, where he was to remain for thirty-five years.

On the island there were among the Baptists ten preaching stations: two houses of worship (Llangefni and New Chapel) and eight private houses (Holyhead, Llanfachreth, White Chapel, Amlwch, Llanfair, Beaumaris, Pencarneddi and Llanerchymedd). There were a few members at each of these places, and all were members of the mother church at Llangefni; that is, all the Baptists in Anglesey formed one church. With Christmas Evans's arrival the Llanfachreth church gave up its independence by joining with Cildwrn (Llangefni) as part of a single multi-branch Baptist church on the island. (Although the official name of the church at Llangefni is Ebenezer, it is more usually called Cildwrn on account of Robert Williams's habit of giving sweets to the people who came to his cottage to do their shopping. It appears that his cottage was a sort of shop for the neighbourhood and that he gave sweets as a *cildwrn* (tip/bribe) to his customers.)

The Baptist societies, though closely connected with each other, were in

Cildwrn Chapel, Anglesey

a lukewarm and chaotic condition, and distracted from their primary task of preaching Christ by theological arguments. From his base at Llangefni Christmas Evans endeavoured to restore order and unity to the whole island.

Llangefni itself was made up of only a few scattered houses, each consisting of just one room, where the members of the family lived and died. In this one room 'all the washing, cooking, baking, weaving, spinning and dyeing were done. Hidden away in corners were the few belongings necessary to live, while under the rafters hung dried fish, salted meat and bacon, and the herbs so necessary to flavour the meals.' Cildwrn chapel, with its small pulpit perched on top of narrow stairs, stood on a bleak and exposed piece of ground, with a good view of the surrounding neighbourhood.

Adjoining the chapel was a small cottage or, more properly, a hut for the minister and his wife. It contained several pieces of ageing and broken furniture: a table, two chairs and a bed that had to be supported by stone slabs. Some of the floorboards had rotted away and in their place lay a pile

Plaque on the wall of Cildwrn Chapel

of bare stones. The door through which the couple entered the cottage was old and decayed, and afforded little shelter from the wind and rain, and the frugal congregation saved the expense of a new door by nailing a tin plate across the bottom of it for added protection against the elements. The roof was so low that the master of the house, who was of commanding stature, could barely stand upright and he often knocked his head. The stable, which housed the preacher's horse, was slightly separated from the cottage.

The first permanent Baptist minister of Cildwrn was Seth Morris from Newcastle Emlyn in the South, a godly and humble man. Matters were going well until he invited Thomas Morris, also from South Wales, to serve as his assistant. 'A more gifted man than the pastor, Thomas Morris's popularity alienated one faction among the members, who saw his success as a threat to their pastor's authority. Polarisation occurred and much acrimony, which led, his faction claimed, to Seth Morris's death in 1785.' After the pastor's death, the field was free for Thomas Morris. He married in 1787, accumulated heavy debts thereafter, and was forced to leave the island. The congregation fell away and the spiritual progress made under the ministry of Seth Morris evaporated, leaving a dismal state of affairs.

It was into this atmosphere of partisanship and conflict, which had driven away many hearers and brought the work into disrepute, that Christmas Evans set about his task with vigour and earnestness. One of his first initiatives was to appoint a day of humiliation for the unhappy divisions in the churches and to fast and pray for God's favour and peace, and the restoration of his blessing. The meeting was held at Llanerchymedd, where the preaching services were usually held. 'We confessed our sins, which had dishonoured the glorious Name, and we had strength in some degree to give our hearts to God, and to lay hold of his covenant. The consequence was, that God's merciful hand was upon us, and we received into fellowship twenty or more persons every year for some time afterwards.' Some who had previously been reticent to get involved were heard to say, 'We will go with you, for we have heard that the Lord is with you.'

Inside Cildwrn Chapel, Anglesey

Catherine Evans's gravestone in the grounds of Cildwrn Chapel

Christmas Evans proceeded to divide the island into four districts so that by preaching in three places every Sabbath, each of the congregations would have at least one Sabbath service a month. During weekdays he preached and held a conference meeting in each district every two weeks. This method he pursued for about twenty years and thereby doubled the number of preaching stations.

He also encouraged each congregation to hold a weeknight *seiat*, or fellowship meeting, believing that 'the particular fellowship of the saints is a special means of strengthening by corporate prayer and delighting together in the things of God. These kinds of meetings are highly valued by those who love the presence of God and the powerful effects of godliness.' He was often away from home for up to five nights a week conducting these meetings. In addition, he found time to attend to church affairs, to visit the needy, and, when the membership increased, he explored the possibility of building chapels to accommodate the growing numbers.

For all his work he was paid only £17 per annum, although this was raised to £30 in later years. He noted his salary without any additional comment, happy as he was to 'serve Anglesey' in poverty.

Occasionally he wrote and printed a small pamphlet, which he was obliged to sell away from home to gain a little extra money for necessary expenses, and which became a mode of conveying knowledge to his countrymen. Of the two principal benefits occasioned by these 'selling' trips, he remarks: 'One was the extension of my ministry, so that I became almost as well known in one part of the Principality as the other; and secondly, [God] gave me the favour and the honour to be the instrument of bringing many to Christ, through all the counties of Wales, from Presteigne to St David's, and from Cardiff to Holyhead. Who will speak against a preacher's poverty, when it thus spurs him to labour in the vineyard?'

From 1792–1826 he served many congregations and preaching stations, but when these became too numerous for him to shepherd single-handedly, he endeavoured to place resident pastors over some of them while remaining as general supervisor over all. Some of the pastors and congregations did not take kindly to this form of imposed government and, as shall be seen, they stirred up considerable trouble for him, which eventually led to his departure from Anglesey.

Chapter 9

In the right direction

During his Anglesey pastorate, whether at home or on a preaching tour, Christmas Evans read constantly, and would take up with delight any interesting volume that came his way, sometimes meditating on it for hours while cutting peculiar marks on his chair with a penknife. At times these meditations were so intense and concentrated that he was oblivious to everything else. After he had learned to read English, he avidly read the books in that language.

Although he read theological works from all schools, his favourite authors were John Owen, the Reformed theologian, whose works he admired to the end of his days; and John Gill, the Baptist minister and biblical scholar. The former helped to shape his theology, the latter influenced his ideas about the exposition of Scripture. He rated Robert Haldane's *Exposition of the Epistle to the Romans* as one of the best commentaries he knew and unhesitatingly recommended it to other ministers. He enjoyed the commentaries of the American scholar Moses Stuart, and one of his most treasured possessions, which he learned to use in both languages when he was about forty, was *A Greek and English Lexicon to the New Testament* by John Parkhurst. In addition, 'The writings of Andrew Fuller modified the rigidity of his earlier Calvinism, and he was very appreciative of the *Essays* of John Foster. As we should expect, he was a great lover and a diligent student of John Bunyan.'

He was eminently a man of one book, the Bible, which he valued as supremely important and beyond the usefulness of all others. To him the Bible was 'a most wonderful book. It came to us from heaven, and is stamped with the Spirit and the character of heaven. It is the sword of God, by which he conquers the nations—the instrument of his grace, by which he renovates the world; it is more than a match for the cunning and prowess of the Prince of Darkness and his hosts.'

He searched the Scriptures for hours in preparation for preaching, and his sermons are full of biblical quotations, sometimes filling whole paragraphs, and 'even that lofty imagery which constituted the peculiar charm of his ministry was ordinarily but an amplification of Scriptural [metaphors] and descriptions'. In a sermon he prepared for the press he describes, with his usual imagery, how he 'trembled' before the Word and how the 'two-edged sword penetrated into my heart'.

His love for the Bible, and hunger for knowledge in general, influenced those who sat under his ministry, as the testimony of David Owen (Brutus), a harsh critic of the Welsh nonconformist pulpit, bears out: 'The congregation of Cildwrn were, while under the oversight of Christmas Evans, very knowledgeable in the Scriptures. They had an excellent grounding in the Word generally, and were able to reason readily and proficiently on the various articles of the Christian faith. They were thirsty and seeking hard after knowledge. They were great readers, with broad understanding. They were faithful, kind and extremely amiable, simple and godly. They were Christmas Evans's people.'

In the early days of his Anglesey ministry, he found it hard to govern the Baptist assemblies with the tact and patience they demanded, tending to be overbearing and too dogmatic in his views. This, along with the opposition that inevitably arises when the Lord begins a work, brought him into conflict with others. His character was attacked and various rumours that cast doubt on the integrity of his purpose began to circulate. One of these rumours alleged that he was paid half a crown for each person he baptised. 'This falsehood he squashed in his own inimitable way. The opportunity arose when he was to baptise the wife of a farmer of some social standing. A large crowd had gathered for the occasion. Lifting up his voice the preacher exclaimed, "They say I receive half a crown for each person I baptise. That is not true. I receive a crown—not half a one. They shall be my crown of joy and rejoicing in the great day."'

With characteristic boldness he was able to answer his critics and continue with his work. Slowly but surely he managed to reintroduce the habit of prayer among the members of his congregations, to establish a form of order under which the churches could operate, and, to some degree, to succeed in restoring public confidence in the Baptist denomination, which had been shattered by 'the Morris affair'.

A household name

With some satisfaction at the progress made on the island Christmas Evans embarked on his second journey to South Wales, preaching along the route as he had done before. On his arrival he found that the religious aspects of the churches and hearers had changed considerably. A dry and critical spirit due to a series of doctrinal contentions that had arisen had replaced the enthusiasm and fervour which marked his previous visit.

The disputes at this time compromised and engaged many of the ministers in the counties of Pembroke, Carmarthen and Cardigan, and produced among the people 'a habit of critical hearing', and a desire to learn more about the 'disputed points'. This censorious way of thinking was certainly not a favourable attitude with which to hear Christmas Evans.

Christmas Evans's expectations for the tour were greatly frustrated, but instead of losing heart he returned home all the more determined to revitalise the church in the North. To his surprise and obvious delight he discovered that while he had been away the Spirit of God had fallen on his people and stirred up within them a deeper interest in religious things, so that the meeting places, usually the district's farms, soon became too small to accommodate the growing numbers attending the services.

Having seen the larger churches in the South, Christmas Evans decided to erect several chapels for his growing congregations, even though there was much ignorance among Baptists about chapel building and sufficient funds were not readily available. Economically it was not a good time to build. The island was in a state of depression, with soaring prices, especially the price of wheat, and fish was the only plentiful food. Many children were severely undernourished and disease was rampant. Nevertheless, at an Association meeting at Ebenezer, Anglesey, in 1794, a resolution was passed that 'Brother Christmas Evans be permitted to collect among the churches for a meeting-house at Amlwch'. With his people's backing the pastor journeyed to the Association in Carmarthenshire, in order to raise the necessary capital.

In 1794, when the annual South-West Baptist Association, comprising about thirty churches, was held on 11–12 June at Felin-foel near Llanelli, there were only two or three Associations in the Principality. Christmas Evans had already preached at the Northern Association in 1791, the first to be held since the single Welsh Association divided, but there are no records of any unusual successes from his labours there. He had attended the Association in the South in 1792 and 1793, but it was in 1794, at Felin-foel, that he became a household name.

Although the distance was some 200 miles, Christmas Evans set out on foot, preaching at various places along the way, and duly arrived on time. The meeting, which drew huge crowds from all over Wales, was held in the open air on a sloping field that commanded an extensive view of the surrounding country. It commenced at 10:00 on Wednesday morning—an 'oppressively hot' summer's day—with three consecutive sermons. Christmas Evans, who was known only to the ministers present and in certain Baptist circles, was to speak last. The first two orators were long and rather tedious and 'the hearers seemed almost stupefied', which may partly be accounted for by the fact that a large proportion of the people in Carmarthenshire could not understand one word of English!

Christmas Evans then rose and stood before the desk: 'His subject was the return of the prodigal son. With an abundant flow of beautiful language, with apt illustrations, and with great fervour and enthusiasm, he described, in a long strain, the mercy of God welcoming the sinner back to his home. The people, immediately after he began, collected together in a compact mass; those that were sitting on the ground at once stood on their feet. And with description after description of the return of the prodigal, the palace, the guest, the sumptuous feast, etc, a strong wave of emotion passed over the congregation; and there were tears and great joy, and loud praise; and these expressions of feeling continued for a long time after the preacher had finished his sermon.'

An eye-witness says that when he had spoken for about fifteen minutes, 'hundreds of the people, who were sitting on the grass, all at once sprang up as if they had been electrified', some weeping, some praising, some leaping and clapping their hands for joy, others praying in the greatest agony of mind. 'He was therefore under the necessity of giving over preaching, but the people kept up the meeting.' For the rest of the day and during the whole night, the voice of rejoicing and prayer was heard in every direction; and the dawning of the next day, awaking the few who had fallen asleep through fatigue, only renewed the heavenly rapture.

Not everyone, though, welcomed this religious excitement. 'Job David, the Socinian,' who was present at the meeting, 'was highly displeased with this American gale,' said the preacher afterwards to a friend; and a learned and judicious Baptist minister observed that he 'hoped he should never see Christmas on the second week in June any more'. But the 'gale' was too strong and too heavenly to be counteracted or frustrated by such criticism. Instead, the outcome of this one sermon in so prominent a setting was that Christmas Evans became one of the most popular and well-known preachers in the Principality.

Every summer Christmas Evans was one of the great preachers at the various Associations in Wales. From the records it appears that he was present at nearly all the meetings and as a result became honoured and loved by the masses, and the very mention of his name created great excitement. Between 1791 and 1836 he preached at the South-Eastern Associations twenty-one times, and at the South-Western Associations thirty-four times, as well as many times in the Northern Association, making in all a total of 163 public Associational sermons, which is more than any other of his countrymen. He has rightly been called 'the man for the whole of Wales'.

In his day and as a result of his labours the Baptist Associations, particularly the one in Anglesey, rose to great prominence and popularity, with the annual conferences becoming memorable occasions. It is true to say that 'he did not visit any part of Wales where he did not meet with some who claimed him as their spiritual father, the Lord having so extensively blessed his travelling ministry for the conversion of souls unto himself.' Several of the most respected ministers that were ever known in the Principality came to the fore during this period and 'He was in some measure, more or less, a blessing to all of them; he undoubtedly contributed to their vigorous and zealous exertions in the cause of religion.' One of these men justly observed, 'There is life and evangelical savour attending Christmas Evans, wherever he is.' 'None of us understand and comprehend the extent of Christmas Evans's usefulness,' said another.

C. H. Spurgeon was moved to comment on how he 'aroused his audiences and flashed truth into their faces'. Spurgeon himself, at an early date in his career, so far succeeded in captivating the Welsh 'that one admiring ancient dame ventured the opinion that the London preacher only needed to be blind of one eye to take rank with Christmas Evans'.

After the 1794 Felin-foel Association, the ministry of Christmas Evans flourished, and the Baptist cause advanced and prospered around him, blossoming 'beneath the genial showers of divine grace, like the garden of the Lord, and the sweet notes of the birds of paradise echoed cheerfully in all the plantations of King Jesus'. All proceeded with heavenly blessing for a few years until, in the words of Christmas Evans, 'a black cloud arose on the churches of the North, and a destructive storm burst from it'.

Heresy

The 'black cloud' that Christmas Evans referred to was a controversy called Sandemanianism that was to shake the Baptist churches of North Wales. It had already spread its 'limping, unbalanced teaching' among the Welsh Methodists in the 1760s, principally through the exhorter John Popkin.

Sandemanianism is a set of doctrines named after one of its chief exponents, the Scottish minister Robert Sandeman (1718–71), who was the son-in-law of John Glas (1695–1773), the founder of the sect; hence its followers are sometimes called Glasites. In accordance with his literal interpretation of Scripture, Glas favoured separation of church and state, and a complete autonomy for each local congregation. In an effort to safeguard the doctrine of justification by faith alone, he redefined faith as a bare intellectual assent to certain facts and discarded the Calvinistic doctrines of assurance and the final perseverance of the saints, as well as the Methodist view of conversion.

Unlike his father-in-law, Sandeman was an aggressive and contentious man, a born polemicist, who made a name for himself when he attacked James Hervey's book *Theron and Aspasio* (1755), a Calvinist evangelical work. He claimed that an intellectual assent to the work of Christ was sufficient for salvation and that all religious feelings or desires were unnecessary and to be shunned. He opposed all direct calls, warnings and invitations to the sinner to believe on Christ, teaching that faith is a mere passive reception of the truth. His main doctrine was that 'the bare death of Jesus Christ, which he finished on the cross, is sufficient, without a deed or a thought on the part of man, to present the chief of sinners spotless before God'.

A third man, notable because of his connection with Sandemanianism, is Archibald McLean (1733–1812), a one-time member of Glas's church. In 1765 he left that sect and embraced Baptist principles. Although he rejected the label 'Sandemanian Baptist', he retained much of the Sandemanian teaching. 'A simple belief in the testimony of God about his Son' was his definition of faith, which he taught was 'an act of the mind and of that alone'.

Although Sandemanians adhered to many of the orthodox Christian doctrines, they held erroneous views on the nature of saving faith, claiming that 'faith in Christ was the revelation of truth to the understanding in which neither the will nor the affections participate; that the faith of Christians and devils differs only in its results, and that these arise from the nature of the truth believed'. Their system, as it relates to the nature of justifying faith, was *the bare belief of the bare truth*. It regarded holy affections and pious exercises as 'works' and neglected the aspects of personal application of the truth to the heart and will. There was no need, in the Sandemanian view, for any sort of conviction of sin, because a mere unmoved acknowledgement of Jesus Christ as the Son of God was sufficient for salvation.

Inevitably Sandeman and his followers were against passionate preaching that excited congregations—the fire and the power of the Spirit were resisted and only the bare facts of the Christian faith, without emotion or warmth, were presented, leaving their hearers cold and unmoved. A spirit of censoriousness and intolerance towards Christians of different persuasions developed, with the effect of dividing and subdividing churches into new communities.

At the time of the controversy Christmas Evans was the most accomplished and popular Baptist preacher in the North. The ablest theologian of that denomination, and one of the main proponents of the Sandemanian heresy, who assisted its spread to many parts of Wales, was John Richard Jones (1765–1822), a Baptist minister at Ramoth. Jones had invited Christmas Evans to Anglesey and then risen with him to become the natural leader of the North Wales Baptists. There is little doubt that he was a man of outstanding ability and, even after his connection with Sandemanianism, 'there was,' according to Christmas Evans, 'a power and greatness in his utterance, which evinced him to be a person possessed of very respectable abilities'.

However, Jones's intelligence was dry and hard, and too deliberately confrontational. 'If,' said he, 'every Bible in the world were consumed, and every word of Scripture erased from my memory, I need be at no loss how to live a religious life, according to the will of God, for I should simply have to proceed in all respects in a way contrary to the popular religionists of this age, and then I could not possibly be wrong.' He was arrogant in tone and, in Christmas Evans's view, 'of a domineering disposition'. He 'could not brook opposition; his equal, much less his superior, could not have lived near him; Caesar-like in this respect, he would rather be a "sovereign in a village than a second in Rome itself"'.

Between 1788 and 1793 Jones fully supported his denomination's efforts to evangelise the North, exhibiting no sign that he was dissatisfied with the revivalist emphasis, and was well on the way to becoming a popular preacher of the type he would later despise. However, towards the end of that period he began to feel increasingly uncomfortable at the emotional scenes generated by revivalistic preaching, and so distanced himself from the 'wild and lunatic passion' and 'the despicable example of the Methodists', as he would later write.

The excesses of the revivalists, Jones believed, had infiltrated the Baptists of the North and within no time he became an outspoken critic of them. 'Now, which is the most dignified way to teach men?' argued Jones. 'Is it by reasoning gravely and in earnest with the understanding and conscience, or by ranting and raving and drivelling and thumping the Bible like a madman? I am absolutely convinced of the irrationality and folly of such offensive practices.' He was 'persuaded that Christianity was a minority religion and in order to retain its purity it had to abstain from appealing to the indifferent multitude'.

Jones devoted untiring energies to the propagation of these new principles and practices in an attempt to revert to the sacraments and rites of the Early Church; and the more firmly he embraced them, the more forthrightly he opposed the Methodist view of salvation, which he claimed was a kind of justification by works, and the revivalism that had for years pervaded the country, especially the ecstatic *jumping* of the congregations. Being a man of learning, he exercised a profound influence within the Baptist denomination in the North. Between the years 1795 and 1798 he successfully infused 'the poisonous draught' into the minds of many of his brethren, both ministers and others, Christmas Evans included.

Many of the churches were slow to act practically according to Jones's principles, so he urged those 'true to the faith' to 'come out of Babylon and separate themselves in order to have unity of spirit, and walk in brotherly love'. Eventually, in the winter of 1798, along with the majority of the Baptists of Merioneth who were under his leadership, he separated himself from the 'Babylonian' Baptists of Wales. Soon churches from all over the North followed his lead.

The division was a heavy blow to a denomination that had barely found its feet, and, as feared, no reconciliation ever took place, while the effects of Sandemanianism on Christmas Evans were devastating.

As cold as ice

The reason for mentioning J. R. Jones at such length is because of the extraordinary influence he had on Christmas Evans. Along with the writings of the Scottish Baptists and Christmas Evans's own 'craving for anything new', it was Jones who was primarily responsible for leading his ministerial colleague into Sandemanianism. Christmas Evans always admired men of strong convictions and forthright views and could be led astray by them if they expressed their beliefs in an eloquent and dogmatic fashion. His admiration for Jones as a theologian, and his readiness to submit to his superior intellect, blinded him to the errors of his teaching, and before long he was 'singing from the same hymn sheet', although in later years he was slow to admit any close attachment to the Sandemanian sect.

Various letters written by Christmas Evans show the depth of his involvement in the Sandemanian heresy and his close alignment with the movement's leader—an alignment that was destined eventually to fall apart as both men were concerned ultimately with different priorities: John Jones with the intricacies of his doctrinal system and in persuading all and sundry that his beliefs were the only ones in agreement with the apostolic practice; and Christmas Evans, naturally warm-hearted and ebullient, with the passionate proclamation of the gospel and the conversion of sinners. However, before their separation, it is clear that Christmas Evans considered following Jones's lead and breaking away from the old Baptists if they did not submit to the Sandemanian viewpoint.

With the movement's rigidity and formality Christmas Evans soon lost the warmth and urgency of soul that had been a hallmark of his ministry. The spiritual enjoyment and zeal for God's glory experienced by him at Lleyn evaporated and his prayer life, usually free and overflowing, was stifled. In line with the Sandemanian spirit, he became hard, censorious and peevish. A spirit of infallibility possessed him. He knew something was wrong and that he had lost something precious, but he did not know what it was or how to regain it. His confidence plummeted, his spiritual life became imbued to an alarming extent with the dryness of the system, and his usefulness as a preacher was seriously curtailed. He suffered in this way for about five years.

Taking a retrospective view of the effects on his own spirit and remarking that 'I shall be in eternity when this comes before the reader's eye', he wrote: 'The Sandemanian heresy affected me so much as to drive away the spirit of prayer for the salvation of sinners. The lighter matters of the kingdom of God pressed heavier upon my mind than the weightier. The power, which gave me zeal and confidence and earnestness in the pulpit for the conversion of souls to Christ, was lost. My heart sank within me, and I lost the witness of a good conscience. On Sunday night, after I had been fiercely and violently condemning errors, my conscience felt ill at ease, and rebuked me because I had lost communion and fellowship with God, and made me feel that something invaluable was now lost and wanting. I would reply that I acted according to the Word. Still it rebuked me, saying that there was something of inestimable value gone. To a very great degree had I lost the spirit of prayer, and the spirit of preaching.'

The effect on Christmas Evans's people as a religious body in the North was devastating. The 'pastor of Anglesey' summarises the effect: 'We lost in Anglesey nearly all those who were accustomed to attend with us; some of them joined other congregations; and, in this way, it pulled down nearly all that had been built up in twelve or fifteen years, and made us appear once again a mean and despicable party in the view of the country.'

There seems to have been only one Baptist minister at that time in

Peniel Chapel erected in 1897 in the centre of Llangefni in memory of Christmas Evans

North Wales known to the public who stood firmly and fearlessly against the prevailing doctrines of Sandemanianism and effectively resisted its influence. His name was Thomas Jones (1769–1850) of Glyn Ceiriog, Denbighshire.

Although his opponents attacked Jones viciously, he did not respond in kind, remaining humble and courteous throughout the controversy, yet vigorous in his determination to uphold the truth of the gospel. In 1802 at the resuscitated Association meeting at Llangefni, he preached so effectively against Sandemanianism that the heresy never recovered. During the final sermon on the Thursday afternoon, as Jones preached from 1 John 2:12, Christmas Evans, obviously gripped by what he heard, cried, 'You know, this Thomas Jones is a whale of a man!' It was after this meeting that Christmas Evans turned his back on the Sandemanian position.

Coupled with the influence of Thomas Jones was Christmas Evans's own conviction that the callousness and severity that characterized Sandemanians were contrary 'to the two tablets of the law and to the kind and gracious nature of the gospel, and to the nature of the graces or fruit of the Holy Spirit'. He complained that the men of Ramoth, who were 'far more like the Pharisee in the parable than the publican', possessed 'no real pleasure in the exercise of religion and walking with God'; dismissed family devotions, which had been practised for years, as unscriptural; opposed prayer meetings, Sunday schools and missionary endeavours, stating that there were no specific instructions concerning them in the New Testament and therefore they should be abolished; and despised everything that savoured of experience and spiritual life.

Religion to them was an external matter 'that did not affect the objectivity of the doctrine of faith and salvation', whereas, in the words of Christmas Evans, 'the spirit of Christ's kingdom is a spirit of prayer, yes, perseverance in prayer; the most important things in Christ's kingdom are righteousness, peace and joy in the Holy Spirit. But certainly that is not the spirit of the Scottish Baptists, rather it is hostility and resentment towards the good who appear like full-blown flowers among them. They have no desire to listen to a sermon or to pray, to seek to save their ungodly neighbours and they have no tear to shed as they see the world lying in ignorance of the knowledge of the only Saviour.' It was this Pharisaical spirit that caused him to reappraise his own views.

Christmas Evans was also challenged by the writings of Andrew Fuller (1754–1815). In 1785 Fuller had published *The Gospel Worthy of all Acceptation*, an evangelical Calvinistic work that provoked criticism from both hyper-Calvinists and Sandemanians. The former accused him of Arminianism and the latter of advocating justification by works. McLean's reply, *The Commission of Christ*, a translation of which was signed on the title page by Christmas Evans, J. R. Jones and Edmund Francis, was challenged by Fuller in an appendix to the 1801 edition of his original work, in which he again emphasized the evangelical doctrine of saving faith.

Christmas Evans read the appendix, and began to re-examine and change his views respecting 'Sandemanian faith'. He then read twice McLean's *Reply* and in some degree reverted to his old beliefs. Soon afterwards Fuller produced a more detailed exposure of the system, called *Strictures on Sandemanianism*, and Christmas Evans, to use his own expression, 'saw the *Rhinoceros* of Edinburgh beginning to give way, notwithstanding the strength and sharpness of his horn, before the *elephant* of Kettering, and confess that faith is of a holy nature'. He understood the scriptural basis of Fuller's argument and became more established in orthodox beliefs.

Both Jones and Fuller, aided by the Spirit of truth, helped Christmas Evans to escape from the 'religious ice-house' of Sandemanianism, but it was a remarkable encounter he had with God that finally sealed his deliverance. He had been trapped in the controversy for about five years, destitute of all religious enjoyment and as cold and hard as ice—'as dry as Gilboa' is how he pictures himself. Then one day, as he travelled by himself up a lonely road near Cadair Idris, he experienced a spiritual refreshing that changed the course of his life. God met with him and a new day dawned. He broke with the 'reformers' and their movement, and reverted to his old warm and powerful revivalism.

He describes what happened and the subsequent blessing in his journal: 'I was weary of a cold heart towards Christ, and his sacrifice and the work of his Spirit—of a cold heart in the pulpit, in secret prayer, and in the study.

For fifteen years previously, I had felt my heart burning within, as if going to Emmaus with Jesus.

'On a day ever to be remembered by me, as I was going from Dolgellau to Machynlleth and climbing up towards Cadair Idris, I considered it to be incumbent upon me to pray, however hard I felt my heart, and however worldly the frame of my spirit was. Having begun in the name of Jesus, I soon felt as it were the fetters loosening, and the old hardness of heart softening, and, as I thought, mountains of frost and snow dissolving and melting within. This engendered confidence in my soul in the promise of the Holy Spirit. I felt my whole mind relieved from some great bondage: tears flowed copiously, and I was constrained to cry out for the gracious visits of God, by restoring to my soul the joy of his salvation;—and that he would visit the churches in Anglesey that were under my care. I embraced in my supplications all the churches of the saints, and nearly all the ministers in the Principality by their names.

'This struggle lasted for three hours; it rose again and again, like one wave after another, or a high flowing tide driven by a strong wind, until my nature became faint by weeping and crying. Thus I resigned myself to Christ, body and soul, gifts and labours—all my life—every day and every hour that remained for me:—and all my cares I committed to Christ. The road was mountainous and lonely, and I was wholly alone, and suffered no interruption in my wrestlings with God.

'From this time, I was made to expect the goodness of God to churches and to myself. Thus the Lord delivered me and the people of Anglesey from being carried away by the flood of Sandemanianism. In the first religious meetings after this, I felt as if I had been removed from the cold and sterile regions of spiritual frost, into the verdant fields of the divine promises. The former striving with God in prayer, and the longing anxiety for the conversion of sinners, which I had experienced at Lleyn, was now restored. I had a hold of the promises of God. The result was when I returned home, the first thing that arrested my attention was, that the Spirit was working also in the brethren in Anglesey, inducing in them a spirit of prayer, especially in two of the deacons, who were particularly importunate that God would visit us in mercy, and render the word of his grace effectual amongst us for the conversion of sinners.'

A turnaround in faith and experience of this magnitude infuriated J. R. Jones, who represented Christmas Evans as a man hunting after applause and paving the way for his own glory and honour. 'I remember the time,' he said accusingly, 'when there was no one as zealous for what he calls the McLeanist tenets as Christmas Evans. But after that, he discovered that it was more advantageous for his popularity and pocket to resort to his previous creed and stick to his old mistress—*hwyl*.' But criticism such as this from his former ally could not deter a man who had been locked for five years inside 'the coldness of death' by the rigidity and hardness of the Sandemanian system.

And so the old fires of love for Christ and the souls of men began to burn again in the heart of Christmas Evans, much to the benefit of the Baptist cause in North Wales. The unbending strictness that observed 'the letter that killeth' was replaced by the Spirit of life, inducing prayer and praise; and his feelings and imagination, stifled and suppressed for too long, were given the free reign they had formerly enjoyed.

Walking with God again

Although the Sandemanian controversy caused considerable harm among the North Wales Baptists, and pulled down what had taken years of hard work to build, it also had a more salutary effect in checking some extravagances that had grown up. Before the dispute, preaching in the North, generally speaking, had deteriorated. Many sermons, with a tendency to ultra-Calvinism, were taken from obscure or short texts and applied with strange spiritualisations. After the controversy the preaching was observed to be less exaggerated in its handling of God's Word, with a more gracious and experimental effect on the hearts of the hearers. The 'old Baptists' became much more 'sober in handling the word of life. The ministers of the gospel aimed more at purifying the heart, by informing the understanding of the truth of God in its glorious harmony, its melting love, and holy tendency.'

These beneficial effects were also apparent in the ministry of Christmas Evans, whose involvement with Sandemanianism forced him to reassess his religious beliefs, which in turn deepened his knowledge and understanding of the true principles of Christianity: 'It shook my old system like an earthquake; so that I was obliged to search all the foundations, and repair some of the gates, and measure the whole by the measuring rod of the truth. It made me re-examine for myself according to the word, into every part of my religion. This enlarged my understanding, and established my mind the more in the truth.

'Were it not for this earthquake, I could not treat of several points of religion in a manner nearly equal to the small degree of power with which I can do it at present. I derived so much blessing from the rise of Sandemanianism, that made me descend into the mine-pit myself by the ropes to examine and see what was in it. It compelled me to prove, search, and see for my own self, what saith the Lord in his holy Scriptures.'

These blessings—a sharpening of his critical skills, a more rigorous intellectual discipline in his attitude towards theology and its tenets, a greater substance and solidity to his preaching—made him well prepared to counter another heresy making inroads into the Baptists of Wales at this time: Sabellianism. He spoke out fearlessly against it, regarding it as both dangerous and divisive, and incurred considerable opposition, especially from some of the brethren in Monmouthshire, where Sabellianism had taken a deep root. In 1802, when requested to write the circular letter of the South-West Baptist Association, held that year at Pen-parc, Cardiganshire, he chose as his subject *Three Equal Persons in the Undivided Essence of the Godhead*, and wrote so effectively that, coupled with his frequent preaching on the subject, the advance of Sabellianism among the Baptists was considerably hampered.

It was about this time, after his 'wrestling with God' near Cadair Idris and his deliverance from Sandemanianism, that he was guided and strengthened on his course by a series of dreams, which are remarkable for their peculiarity. These visions of the night, many of which he believed to be divinely inspired, were often as vivid, imaginative and dramatic as his sermons and invariably exalted 'the great and blessed Saviour' and his victory over Satan.

In one, he found himself 'at the gate of hell and, standing at the threshold, I saw an opening, beneath which there was a vast sea of fire in wave-like motion. Looking at it, I said: "What infinite virtue there must have been in the blood of Christ to have quenched, for His people, these awful flames!" Overcome with the feeling, I knelt down by the walls of hell, saying, "Thanks be unto Thee, O Great and Blessed Saviour, that Thou hast dried up this terrible sea of fire!"

'Whereupon Christ addressed me, "Come this way, and I will show thee how it was done." Looking back, I beheld that the whole sea had disappeared. Jesus passed over the place, and said, "Come, follow me."

'By this time, I was within what I thought were the gates of hell, where there were many cells, out of which it was impossible to escape. I found myself within one of these, and anxious to make my way out. Still I felt wonderfully calm, as I had only just been conversing with Jesus, and because He had gone before me, although I had now lost sight of Him. I got hold of something, with which I struck the corner of the place in which I stood, saying, "In the name of Jesus, open!" and it instantly gave way; so I did with all the enclosures, until I made my way out into the open field. Whom should I see there but brethren, none of whom, however, I knew, except a good old deacon, and their work was to attend to a nursery of trees; I joined them, and laid hold of a tree, saying, "In the name of Jesus, be thou plucked up by the root!" And it came up as if it had been a rush. Thence I went forth, as I fancied, to work miracles, saying, "Now I know how the apostles wrought miracles in the name of Christ."'

After fourteen years of ministry on the island a formal application for a preaching licence for the 'pastor of Anglesey' was submitted to the Beaumaris magistrates. It was dated 5 October 1805, and signed by twelve Cildwrn members.

On his visits to Liverpool, Bristol and other parts of England, where he spoke in the Welsh churches, he was 'begged earnestly' by his English friends to preach in their churches, in 'broken English', which 'induced me to set about the matter in earnest, making it a subject of prayer, for the aid of the Spirit, that I might be, in some measure, a blessing to the English friends, for there appeared some sign that God now called me to this department of labour in his service. I never succeeded in anything for the good of others, without making it a matter of prayer. My English preaching was very broken and imperfect in point of language; yet, through the grace of Jesus Christ, it was made in some degree useful at Liverpool, Bristol, and some other places.'

Christmas Evans regarded the services he rendered to his friends in England as insignificant. However, it is true to say that the English sermons possessed 'the same energy of thought and the same boldness of imagery as those in Welsh; but in the power of his peculiar delivery, they were inevitably inferior. His brethren in England were delighted with his performances and said it was "no wonder the Welsh were warm under such preaching"; but his language was broken and hesitant, and they could scarcely have any conception of his animation and energy when he spoke in his vernacular tongue.' He admitted some years later that if he had studied the English language 'attentively and perseveringly', he would have been able to overcome many of his difficulties.

A covenant with God

Towards the end of the first decade of the nineteenth century Christmas Evans entered into a solemn covenant with God, in which he dedicated himself wholly to God and his service. It is a wonderful example of the strength and simplicity of his faith, his unwavering hope in the grace of God, and of the humility of spirit in which he lived; and was made, as he says, 'in hope and confidence in Christ, and nearness to God, under a deep sense of the evil of my own heart and in dependence upon the infinite grace and merit of the Redeemer'. Many regard the covenant as among the most intimate in Christian literature.

I. I give my soul and body unto thee, Jesus, the true God, and everlasting life—deliver me from sin and from eternal death, and bring me into life everlasting. Amen.—C. E.

II. I call the day, the sun, the earth, the trees, the stones, the bed, the table and the books to witness that I come unto thee, Redeemer of sinners, that I may obtain rest for my soul from the thunders of guilt and the dread of eternity. Amen.—C. E.

III. I do, through confidence in thy power, earnestly entreat thee to take the work into thine own hand, and give me a circumcised heart, that I may love thee, and create in me a right spirit, that I may seek thy glory. Grant me that principle which thou wilt own in the day of judgement, that I may not then assume pale facedness and find myself a hypocrite. Grant me this, for the sake of thy most precious blood. Amen.—C. E.

IV. I entreat thee, Jesus, the Son of God, in power grant me, for the sake of thy agonising death, a covenant interest in thy blood which cleanseth; in thy righteousness, which justifieth; and in thy redemption, which delivereth. I entreat an interest in thy blood, for thy blood's sake and a part in thee, for thy name's sake, which thou hast given among men. Amen.—C. E.

V. O Jesus Christ, Son of the living God, take for the sake of thy cruel death, my time, and strength, and the gifts and talents I possess; which, with a full purpose of heart, I consecrate to thy glory in the building up of thy church in the world, for thou art worthy of the hearts and talents of all men. Amen.—C. E.

VI. I desire thee my great high priest, to confirm by thy power from thy high court, my usefulness as a preacher, and my piety as a Christian, as two gardens nigh to each other; that sin may not have place in my heart to becloud my confidence in thy righteousness, and that I may not be left to any foolish act that may occasion my gifts to wither, and rendered useless before my life ends. Keep thy gracious eye upon me, and watch over me, O my Lord, and my God for ever! Amen.—C. E.

VII. I give myself in a particular manner to thee, O Jesus Christ the Saviour, to be preserved from the falls into which many stumble, that thy name (in thy cause) may not be blasphemed or wounded, that my peace may not be injured, that thy people may not be grieved, and that thine enemies may not be hardened. Amen.—C. E.

VIII. I come unto thee, beseeching thee to be in covenant with me in my ministry. As thou didst prosper Bunyan, Vavasor Powell, Howel Harris, Rowland and Whitefield, O do thou prosper me. Whatsoever things are opposed to my prosperity, remove them out of the way. Work in me everything approved of God, for the attainment of this. Give me a heart 'sick of love' to thyself, and to the souls of men. Grant that I may experience the power of thy word before I deliver it, as Moses felt the power of his own rod before he saw it on the land and waters of Egypt. Grant this, for the sake of thine infinitely precious blood, O Jesus my hope, and my all in all! Amen.—C. E.

IX. Search me now and lead me in plain paths of judgement. Let me discover in this life what I am before thee, that I may not find myself of another character, when I am shown in the light of the immortal world, and open my eyes in all the brightness of eternity. Wash me in thy redeeming blood. Amen.—C. E.

X. Grant me strength to depend upon thee for food and raiment, and to make known my requests. O let thy care be over me as a covenant-privilege betwixt thee and myself, and not like a general care to feed the ravens that perish, and clothe the lily that is cast into the oven; but let thy care be over me as one of thy family, as one of thine unworthy brethren. Amen.—C. E.

XI. Grant, O Jesus, and take upon thyself the preparing of me for death, for thou art God; there is no need, but for thee to speak the word. If possible, thy will be done; leave me not long in affliction, nor to die suddenly, without bidding adieu to my brethren, and let me die in their sight, after a short illness. Let all things be ordered against the day of removing from one world to another, that there be no confusion nor disorder, but a quiet discharge in peace. O grant me this, for the sake of thine agony in the garden! Amen—C. E.

XII. Grant, O blessed Lord, that nothing may grow and be matured in me, to occasion thee to cast me off from the service of the sanctuary, like the sons of Eli; and for the sake of thine unbounded merit, let not my days be longer than my usefulness. O let me not be like lumber in a house in the end of my days,—in the way of others to work. Amen.—C. E.

XIII. I beseech thee, O Redeemer, to present these my supplications before the Father: and O inscribe them in thy book with thine own immortal pen, while I am writing them with my mortal hand, in my book on earth. According to the depths of thy merit, thine undiminished grace, and thy compassion, and thy manner unto people, O attach thy name, in thine upper court, to these unworthy petitions; and set thine amen to them, as I do on my part of the covenant. Amen.—CHRISTMAS EVANS, Llangefni, Anglesey, April 10, 18—.

Referring to this solemn covenant and the sense of security it brought him, he subsequently wrote: 'I felt a happy degree of peace and tranquillity of mind, like unto a poor man who had been brought under the protection of the royal family, and who had an annual settlement for life made upon him; from whose dwelling the painful dread of poverty and want had been for ever banished away; or like the brood under the wing of the hen. This is to dwell under the shadow of the Almighty, and hide beneath the shadow of his wings until every calamity is over past.'

By 1812 the membership of the Anglesey church had risen to about 385, with many more occasional listeners. With these larger congregations Christmas Evans turned his thoughts to church discipline and how best to encourage members to live according to their high calling. Private sins should be dealt with according to Matthew 18:15–18, he advised, while public sins were a matter for the whole church. If the transgression was serious enough, excommunication should be exercised, without any possibility of restoration, for 'there is no hope of changing a wolf into a lamb even after forty years of discipline'.

In a letter of 1813 he listed four of the most common faults: a factious spirit, a disregard for church meetings, a lack of love among the membership, and impropriety. He was quite prepared to expel any member who was guilty of these sins.

In 1811 Christmas Evans had complained about a lack of dependence on the Holy Spirit among preachers, who were tempted to 'go through a sermon as a child reads its lesson, without the brightness of divine glory'. On the one hand, the great danger was to preach Christ 'without spiritual feeling', coldly and lifelessly, or to listen to the gospel 'in a worldly spirit'; on the other hand, the great need of the hour was for God to pour out his power upon the church as he had done at Llanfachreth in 1805 and two years later at Brynsiencyn, where many had been awakened to eternal life. Little did the pastor of Anglesey realise that his yearnings for a deeper experience of God's grace in the churches under his care and for the fields to be made 'white unto harvest' were about to be satisfied.

Revival

Although the prospects for a revival looked bleak in 1812–13,
Christmas Evans continued to preach with zeal and energy until, in
1814, a spirit of prayer descended on the churches, creating a deeper
solemnity towards the things of God, especially among some of his
deacons, and a new earnestness for spiritual prosperity. The fervour and
devotion of the congregations, previously lukewarm, were restored and
many were invigorated with new life.

At the beginning of the revival Christmas Evans felt compelled to visit
the South, leaving the responsibility for the Anglesey church in the hands of
his assistant preachers. Robert Williams was appointed to take charge of
Cildwrn. 'On one midweek evening,' Williams observes, 'there broke out a
revival so powerful and general that there were, before the close of the
service, in Ebenezer, many on their knees in prayer, crying out for mercy
and clear signs that the Spirit of the living God was applying the ministry to
the hearts of the hearers unto salvation; and by the time of Mr Evans's
return from his visit to the South, the congregation had multiplied greatly
and a number of candidates were requesting baptism.'

Within two years (1814–15) the eleven preaching places on the island
belonging to the Baptists increased to twenty-one; 600 converts were added
to the several branches of the church for which Christmas Evans was
responsible, bringing the total to more than 1000; at Cildwrn, where
'eighty members were added in the course of a few months', a gallery was
built in order to double the number who could attend the chapel; men of
like mind arose to assist him in the ministry; several new chapels were
erected to accommodate the larger congregations; and 'The voice of joy
and praise was heard, because God was again building up the shattered
walls of his church.'

The revival in Anglesey was part of the growth and blessing experienced
by the Baptist denomination during the years 1790–1815, when
consolidation occurred with some 10,000 new converts, an expansion
unthinkable a century earlier. 'Showers of blessing regularly fell on the
churches; they fell like the showers of nature, in a sovereign way and quite

invincibly. The awakening would affect scores in a short time, causing them to shake, weep and cry out "What must I do to be saved?" That would be accompanied by the spirit of intense prayer and seriousness. Sometimes hundreds would be added to single churches during a year. More of God's work is achieved during a single Sabbath of awakening than in years of preaching.'

Such a revival in the religious life of the Welsh people, achieved by the faithful and anointed preaching of the gospel, caused Christmas Evans, a few years later, to write, 'Perhaps no other nation has ever been won over more totally to the hearing of the gospel. Meeting houses have been built in all corners of the land and most of the common people, nearly all of them in fact, regularly congregate to listen.' Thus the Baptists, revived and renewed, and somewhat removed from their old exclusivism, became part of the movement of Dissent that would, by mid-century, not only become the dominant form of Welsh Christianity, but would also transform the religious, social and cultural life of the Welsh people.

During the revival in Anglesey some remarkable instances occurred, such as the following. It was about 1815 that Christmas Evans became acquainted with a respectable young man named Parry from Bangor, who had been brought up in Oxford and prepared for the ministry in the Church of England. Having completed his education he was about to be ordained by the bishop, who was favourably disposed to him, when he approached Christmas Evans at Llangefni, 'apparently under deep conviction, and appeared dead to all earthly objects, as if the eternal world and its important realities, had absorbed his whole soul and body'. His reason for approaching the pastor of Anglesey was to be baptised by him in the river. After questioning the prospective candidate, whose views on baptism were perfectly scriptural, 'I persuaded him to return home without being baptised.'

Christmas Evans continues the story: 'He came to me afterwards on four different occasions, and on the fifth visit, I did all in my power to advise him to return home, and comply with his parents' intentions, urging him as a reason the expense they had incurred in training him up for the ministry of the Episcopal Church. To this he replied, "Oh what an unhappy man I am! Brought up by my parents to earn a livelihood by false preaching, for

Ruined chapel at Brynteg, probably built by Christmas Evans

which I have neither gift nor spirit! Oh that they had brought me up a tinker! I would prefer that."

'He had now commenced undressing himself, with a view to change his clothes for baptism: I endeavoured again with all my power of reasoning (with what propriety I cannot say) to prevail upon him to relinquish the thought and obey his parents, for I could not find him clear in his knowledge of the righteousness of Christ, as the only foundation of a sinner's acceptance with God. This address succeeded so far that he buttoned his clothes; but the next moment unbuttoned them again, uttering these expressions with all solemnity as of another world: "Oh, my parents will not accompany me to the other side of death, and they will not answer for my disobedience in the judgement to come!"

'Here I could not deny him any longer;—"Come down to the river," said I, "and I will baptise you at your own request." Accordingly, we repaired to the river opposite to Ebenezer meeting-house. I read the account of Christ's baptism, and prayed, and went with the young man into the river, without any earthly spectator whatever, but my wife. When he came up out of the water, he appeared as if he had cast off some heavy burden from his shoulders, and his countenance assumed fresh cheerfulness. He said, in the English language, *"Oh Lord! accept this poor sacrifice of mine."* He returned to the house to change his clothes and to take some refreshments; and went his way rejoicing towards Bangor, having offered a sacrifice of obedience upon a watery altar in Llangefni brook.'

Christmas Evans only saw Parry once after his baptism, and that was in

Expensive china statuette of Christmas Evans in the museum in Llangefni

the parish of Llanllyfni, where he was curate. 'For some years he lived morally and circumspectly, and always conducted himself affectionately towards the Baptists', but 'he had no talent for preaching, and his mind was much exercised that he sustained an office whilst he possessed neither spirit nor skill to perform its duties'. At length he resigned from the curacy and the ministry altogether, and 'betook himself to school-keeping for his support'.

After the revival the duties connected with so many branches of the church increased considerably. The principal management of affairs fell on Christmas Evans, including the oversight of the construction of new places of worship and the procurement of funds for the work; his itinerant ministry became more arduous as he attempted to consolidate and teach the growing numbers under his care; and all cases of church discipline were dealt with by him, a time-consuming and often thankless task.

There were ordained ministers and other auxiliaries to assist him in the administration of Christian ordinances, but these twenty-eight preachers, all of whom arose during the course of Christmas Evans's ministry on the island, were natives of Anglesey and committed to other occupations and worldly businesses, and therefore could not spare the time to offer more than a token assistance. They were also young and inexperienced, needing to be trained and encouraged themselves and, in the course of their duties, heavily dependent on Christmas Evans for guidance. An administrative meeting with these preachers, plus one representative from each branch, was held on the first Tuesday of every month, in rotation, at several of the places of worship. It followed a public preaching service, which was conducted on the Monday night. The meetings were generally productive, 'and glorious times they often had together—the Lord was with them, and much good was done in his name'.

Politics

Several of the churches, even after the revival, still suffered under the chilling influence of Sandemanianism—an influence that lasted in one form or another for the next fifteen years. Particularly during his early Anglesey ministry, obstacles to the work arose in the form of some individuals unnecessarily meddling in the political affairs of Wales, and the desire of others to emigrate to America in order to secure more prosperous futures. It was at this point, during the very poor harvests of 1799–1801, when food was both scarce and expensive, that Christmas Evans, in a letter to John Williams, who had earlier emigrated to America, expressed his desire to follow his friend to the 'land full of mercies where life is easy'.

However, as the economic climate improved, he became more settled and the desire to leave the Principality disappeared. In fact, in later years, both these hindrances to the gospel—emigration and politics—which contributed much to weaken the churches in Anglesey and to dampen the spiritual ardour of the ministers who were ensnared by them, greatly annoyed Christmas Evans, who opposed anything that interfered with the simple preaching of Christ. He called 'these two talkative and gifted gentlemen, Mr Politician and Mr Going-to-America, alias Mr Love-Riches', and accused them of 'cooling religious zeal, depriving professors of the spirit of prayer, and at length ending in total apostasy', and of causing 'much mischief in the churches'. 'Few of those who went to America,' he claimed, 'have been of much comfort and usefulness in that country.'

Christmas Evans never engaged in violent political discussion, and was perhaps the most politically inactive of all the Baptist leaders, refusing to be sidetracked by pursuits that were not compatible with his holy calling. Instead of fighting 'battles political', he urged his colleagues to 'set aside some time each week to pray together for the success of the gospel and other worthy causes, such as the health of the king and stability of the kingdom, so that we may live quietly under its rule'. 'It appears clearly to be the duty of all,' he wrote in a letter to one of the island's magistrates on 4 March 1817, 'to humble ourselves before the throne of the Almighty, imploring his mercy instead of imbibing a spirit of disaffection against our civil rulers.'

Along with the majority of Welsh Baptists, who had been strongly conservative for a century and a half, he was 'afraid of being associated in the least manner with those who would threaten their fragile and uncertain civil rights', and, when opportunity arose, would forthrightly speak out in favour of the king: 'May the whole world know that the Baptists of Great Britain submit, for conscience's sake, to the higher authorities (Romans XIII). We are bound to speak respectfully of the king, to pray for him, to pay tribute to him willingly: this is the duty of every true Christian.'

In spite of his 'political shyness', he did speak out against the French Revolution (1789)—a revolution that 'struck terror into his heart'—for a considerable length of time. It seems that the majority of Welsh Baptists were extremely anxious about the prospects of violent revolution, especially as they were dependent in some instances on industrial leaders and their officials. He dreaded Bonaparte and his 'company of terrible thieves' because they had 'killed the royalty and nobility of France in order to snatch and grab possessions for themselves'. 'The fate of France,' he declared, 'was a warning to those who insisted on upholding radicalism, for radicalism went hand in hand with atheism.' The last thing he wanted was a similar revolution in Wales.

Foremost among these political protagonists was the Baptist minister Morgan John Rhys (1760–1804), a 'strange and complex man' in whom 'the spirit of rebellion was very strong', according to Christmas Evans, who also accused his old friend of leading 'many to speak disparagingly of their religious and civil privileges'. He emigrated to America, the Promised Land in his eyes, in 1794.

Although Christmas Evans was not unduly concerned about the departure of Rhys, he was sorry to lose his 'beloved brother' John Williams (1768–1825), whom he had ordained as minister of Garn in 1791. Williams was influenced by the unrest caused by the French Revolution and in 1795 emigrated to New York with his brother. According to Christmas Evans, he was one of the few emigrants who exercised a useful ministry in America.

During his busy ministry, which included almost constant travelling and preaching, he still managed to apply himself to that time-consuming occupation of writing for the press. His output was varied and valuable, ranging from letters and articles to expositions and sermons—he wrote eight Association letters, eight books and three sermons between 1800 and 1815—and he is regarded as 'the most literary of all the great preachers of Wales'. His *Works* were gathered together and edited by Owen Davies, Caernarfon, and published in three substantial volumes (over 2000 pages) in 1898. He also wrote while at Cardiff about 200 sermons on various subjects, which were published in numbers, and thirty numbers were issued from the press before his death.

These books, many of which were sold all over Wales, together with his preaching journeys, made him very well known and popular throughout the Principality. The love and warmth extended to him at the great Association meetings prove the genuine affection in which he was held. At these meetings, where for thirty years he was usually the third and main preacher, men such as John Elias, a frequent hearer, sat 'with his whole form in motion'. On one of these occasions at Llangefni, Elias and his wife were sitting in the crowd listening to Christmas Evans, who had captivated the huge congregation. The sounds of praise and weeping were heard as the preacher ascended to the heights of religious fervour and Elias was seen lifting his handkerchief to his eyes to wipe away the tears of joy.

His catholic spirit, so opposed to sectarianism, especially after his deliverance from Sandemanianism, meant that he was often engaged to preach at the large gatherings of other denominations, such as the Methodists, who took so much delight in claiming him as their own that the Baptists feared his removal to that body. However, it was for his own denomination that he worked tirelessly, promoting the Associations, held annually in Anglesey, to as great a height as any other Association in the Principality—it certainly became through his efforts as large and influential as the older ones in the South and as popular as the Calvinistic Methodists, and gave the Baptists a name and place among the bodies of North Wales, as well as an important part in the 'Nonconformist tide that was sweeping through Wales'. 'There is a very heavenly glow over our assemblies in the North,' said Christmas Evans to Thomas Thomas, minister of Nantglyn, on 20 January 1812, 'so that they are enjoying an abundant unction, and there are signs that they are being especially blessed to raise the character of the [Baptist] cause in the country.'

To further the Association's cause, when he travelled south in the summer, he returned with seven or eight of the ablest preachers in Wales, with whom he engaged in uplifting conversations and in this way became familiar with the work of God in many other parts of the Principality. During the course of their stay, he treated his guests 'with a respect and consideration that frequently astonished them', and in return they often spent three to four weeks touring the North. This practice he continued for thirty-three years.

With the help of these able ministers the Baptist cause in Anglesey flourished and, after the deadness of Sandemanianism, the life, vigour and unity of the churches was the ground of much praise and thanksgiving from their pastor, whose own ministry 'blossomed as the rose'. Many opportunities for preaching the gospel were arising, often beyond the boundaries of his native Wales, and his usefulness in the kingdom of God was becoming more and more apparent. There were arduous and self-sacrificing days ahead though, as the revival, with its influx of new converts, meant that larger and more expensive places of worship were needed on the island to accommodate them. The responsibility for their construction rested on the shoulders of Christmas Evans, and developed into one of the heaviest and most stressful burdens of his ministerial career.

Chapter 17

'Begging' journeys

Christmas Evans now had the extra 'obligation' of paying for the new chapels that were being built on the island—an obligation that continually pressed on his heart and mind and significantly increased his labours, especially as it appears that he was the only man responsible for financing the constructions. 'The usual procedure was to open a meeting place in a certain neighbourhood, in a farmhouse or barn, and, after securing a regular congregation, to plan building a more permanent chapel. When a convenient site had been found, it was the responsibility of the preacher, Christmas himself more often than not, to secure a loan.'

The money for construction was lent on the integrity of his name and that of a friend, sometimes without his consent, thus making him personally responsible for repaying the loan. Within two or three years either the interest was due or the full amount demanded, placing the pastor of Anglesey under considerable pressure.

In order to meet these debts, which his own people had incurred but were either unwilling or too poor to pay anything towards, he visited once a year the stronger and more affluent churches in South Wales or England, with the express purpose of raising money. These special and exhausting 'begging' journeys, as some have called them, were usually undertaken in winter, when the travelling conditions were particularly difficult; they lasted from between six weeks and two months, and were always on horseback. It must also be remembered 'that his constitution was one of the most unhappily formed—exposing him to all the horrors of a most excitably nervous temperament, as well as to all the inconvenience of a most capricious appetite; add to this, that he was at all times incapable of taking any efficient care of himself in dress, in health, or in travelling arrangements; and it will be easily discerned that in every long journey he endured two or three martyrdoms'.

The distress he experienced over these debts is best understood from his own comments: 'I humbly believe that the troubles of our missionaries in India, or any other part of the world, were not so great as those I had to bear

Model of Christmas Evans preaching at museum in Llangefni

with the debts of places of worship; and, moreover, they had not, in the meantime, to care for their own support, as I had during all the time I was in Anglesey; for the London Committee cared for them.' He worked hard to establish a penny-a-week contribution to help the cause, but admits, 'I did not succeed well in it.' Disconsolate and in great need, he poured out his heart to God: 'In the depth of night, I have wrestled in prayer, and entreated God to preserve his cause from disgrace. The promises of the God of Jacob, in support of his cause, were often of great comfort to my soul. I would examine the promises which involve the care of God for his own glory, and would take and spread them before him in prayer, until, sometimes, I felt as confident as if I had seen the whole debt paid.'

During his winter journeys to South Wales, and his summer trips to the annual Associations, he read and meditated on the Word of God with such intensity that sometimes he lost all consciousness of what was going on around him. Once his thirsty horse wandered off the road into a nearby river to drink, before leisurely devouring the long grass that was floating on the surface. Christmas Evans, unaware that the animal had strayed from the intended path or that the water was nearly up to the top of his boots, carried on reading until a chapel-goer alerted him to his watery surroundings.

With delight he used to relate a story that highlights the hazardous nature of the itinerant ministry. 'In some parts of the country, when it was felt desirable to extend the household accommodation, it was done by making a "wattle and daub" addition to the cottage. The apartment thus erected was, in this instance, fixed upon for the "prophet's chamber". It was so small that a "prophet" of our preacher's stature could not fully extend himself in it without an undue pressure of the feet against the decaying fence work, which barely enclosed him from the road. He was woken in the morning by the rumbling of a cart, which sounded dangerously near, and, to his horror, he found that his protruding foot had narrowly escaped a very disagreeable collision.'

While in the South he preached for over an hour at least once every weekday and twice on Sundays. In all, if his summer excursions are included, he travelled from North to South Wales and back *forty times*, making him one of the principal links between Christians throughout the Principality. He notes that he did not know of another minister, even among the Methodists, who had made the journey more than *fifteen times*. It has been calculated that during his ministry in Anglesey he was away from home for a total of seven years and preached for nearly three thousand hours.

Often, as a result of these journeys, a church was planted or a new preaching station opened, and the flagging spirits of ministers and members were invigorated with new vision and purpose. At Aberystwyth, where he ministered regularly on his travels, he was a channel of great blessing. After preaching there on 23 July 1815, John James, the minister in that town, wrote in his diary: 'Christmas Evans preached and there was much unction—more unction than I have seen on a sermon in Ab. for 18 or 20 years.'

Some churches welcomed him annually and were prepared to support his cause. Others objected to his visits, regarding them as irregular and too frequent, and complaining that if he wanted to build *so many* places of worship, he should wait until the people of Anglesey could finance their own projects, instead of begging in the South. They argued, albeit unconvincingly, that they were poor themselves, with their own chapels to maintain, and, because of the 'hard times' they were experiencing, did not possess the means to contribute. These objectors did not deter Christmas Evans. He either ignored them altogether and carried on regardless, or won them over with tact, kindness and eloquence.

The way he collected money on these journeys is of interest though by no means original. After he had concluded the ordinary service, he preached again, with as much zeal and earnestness as before, on the pressing needs of the churches in the North. He then took off his hat and went and stood by the door. As the congregation filed out he held out his hat to receive contributions, which were usually very small. This method he employed for many years until finally, due to the pressures of the work, he delegated a friend to take his place at the door, but never without an apology to the congregation lest it be thought he was disrespectful or inattentive to the generosity of others.

His usual practice when coming to a new neighbourhood was to learn as much as possible about the place and then use the information to his own advantage. On one occasion, when he entered a remote district, he learned that the area was notorious for sheep stealing, so when the time came to urge the crowd to contribute, he spoke animatedly about this crime, saying that in such a large congregation it was certain that some of the perpetrators were present. He addressed the thieves solemnly and implored them *not* to give their *filthy lucre*. The result was dramatic. Those who had no money quickly borrowed from their neighbours so that, it is said, not one person left the meeting without making a contribution!

These 'begging' journeys are not only examples of his dedication to the Baptist cause in Anglesey, but also reminders of his own poverty. He was so poor that some have conjectured that his wife Catherine must have inherited money on which they both lived. One of the causes of his poverty was the frugality of the Welsh, who loved to hear the most eloquent and powerful preachers, but at the time did little to support them.

Usually Christmas Evans was content with his meagre salary, which was supplemented by itinerant fees, but there were occasions when, after preaching, he did not receive enough even to cover his expenses. On one of these occasions, a poor old lady spoke up: 'Well, Christmas Evans, *bach*, I hope you will be paid at the resurrection; you have given us a wonderful sermon.' 'Yes, yes, Shan *fach*,' replied the preacher, 'no doubt of that, but what am I to do till I get there? And there's the old white mare that carries me, what will she do? For her there will be no resurrection.' Sometimes, in order to increase his income, he advertised his sermons and booklets from the pulpit after preaching.

Looking back over half a century of 'travelling, preaching and collecting', and having 'gained nothing of this world's goods', although he thought he had 'endured more toil of body and mind than a dozen of my contemporaries in the ministry', he could see how God had turned all things for good: 'I have nothing to depend upon but the kindness of my brethren, as the Lord may prompt them. In the face of all this, I have reason to be thankful that the spiritual blessings, which I have received, have counterbalanced all the difficulties that I have experienced. It is a matter of wonder to me that my straitened circumstances have been a sort of incentive to my usefulness throughout Wales, as I have been frequently obliged to travel, mainly on account of my own poverty.'

Bitter wrangling

Although the Sandemanian spirit still influenced the lives of some of the Baptist congregations in Anglesey, causing their pastor no little distress and in many ways obstructing the advancement of religion on the island, it was another dispute, called by Christmas Evans 'Wesleyanism', that dominated his attention during the opening years of the nineteenth century. This controversy caused agitation throughout the Principality.

During these years some itinerant Wesleyan preachers, including Edward Jones, an enthusiastic and very effective missionary from Manchester, under the auspices of the Wesleyan Methodist conference in London, started to propagate their doctrines in Welsh in the North with determination and energy. By the close of 1804 most of the northern counties had been visited by them. They met with phenomenal success. The introduction of the Wesleyan preachers, whose aim was to establish Wesleyan Methodism in Welsh-speaking areas, recognising that the native language was the most effective medium for the spread of their doctrines, renewed the controversy over Arminianism, especially concerning the extent of the atonement. This controversy raged in the pulpit and the press for the next thirty years.

Christmas Evans was by no means guiltless in the controversy and, when the contentions were at their fiercest, his 'sword was as bloody as any in the whole of Wales'. In recounting the theological movements in Wales during the nineteenth century, the Calvinistic minister Owen Thomas, an authority on the history and development of preaching in Wales, remarked, 'We have heard many say that Christmas Evans at this time, could hardly preach a sermon without showering Wesleyanism with derision.' His North Wales Associational letter of 1806 illustrates this point with jarring clarity: Wesley's system, he wrote, 'is extremely frightening. It is a black toad, scaby in the passion of its poison, affecting all the sweet flowers in the garden of the Bible. Beware of it as you would beware a snake in the grass, dear brethren, for it contains a multiplicity of error.'

Christmas Evans went further than the moderate Calvinists, who believed that the atonement was sufficient for all but applied only to the elect, when he upheld the view of perfect equality between the death of Christ and the number of elect. 'The essential purpose of his death,' he said, 'was to bear the sins of particular persons and to make atonement for particular persons.' Such a high-Calvinistic stance caused uneasiness among his supporters and led him into a fierce debate with the Methodist leader, Thomas Jones of Denbigh.

Christmas Evans was the first to go into print against the translated works of John Wesley. He published several 'extremely Calvinistic' books. In 1811, in response to the growing numbers of 'moderate Calvinists', he gave further expression of his Calvinistic orthodoxy in the tract *Particular Redemption*, which was intended far more to counteract moderatism than the Arminian view of redemption. It is a brief and somewhat carelessly written attempt to determine exactly what constitutes the particularity for which he argues.

In the tract he introduced 'commercial metaphors', believing in a kind of 'quantitative calculus of the atonement, which held that it was exactly, mathematically equivalent to the amount needed to save the elect'. In other words, 'for Christ's redemption to have been all embracing, he would have had to have suffered quantitatively greater pain on the cross. Oh, the amount of infinite suffering Jesus bore when he took upon himself the curse we deserved, and that curse being equal to the number and weight of our sins in the minutest detail!' Christmas Evans exclaimed.

When he reviewed the controversy Christmas Evans admitted that 'the first intimation given in a printed form in Wales of an atonement *equal* in weight and value to the amount of crime, and not an atonement corresponding with the dignity of the divine person who gave it, was hinted in a small pamphlet of mine, published some years ago. I regret the word *equal* in the above connection.'

Eight years after *Particular Redemption* was published, Thomas Jones, in an appendix to his *Discourses on Redemption* (Denbigh, 1819), was unnecessarily reproachful towards Christmas Evans, heavily condemning his extreme and 'commercial' opinions, and calling them '*constructive* blasphemy'.

Jones's book was published in mid-October 1819. At the time, Christmas Evans was preaching in Denbighshire, where he saw the book advertised. He read a summary of its contents and the intended criticism of his own work on *Particular Redemption*. Thinking the book had not yet been issued, he immediately wrote to Jones from his lodging house in Llangollen on 18 October, begging him 'to wait until you see me early next week in Denbigh. I do not uphold the way of reasoning I adopted in that booklet, i.e., that of weights and measures, which inclined to set a limit to what was limitless, limitless in itself. These days I am revising the subject and see reason to renounce completely that system of weights and measures which, perhaps, grieved you deeply.'

By the time Christmas Evans called to see Jones, he had read the criticisms in the appendix of his book and appeared quite happy with them. According to Jones, their two meetings—a second meeting took place on the following Monday, 1 November 1819—were extremely amicable.

On his return, men who had an interest in prolonging any supposed disagreement, Baptist preachers in Denbigh most likely, persuaded Christmas Evans that Jones had treated him unfairly in his *Discourses* and that he should defend his former high-Calvinistic position. Christmas Evans should have been wise and strong enough to ignore their criticisms; instead, a booklet from his hand soon appeared with the provocative title: *Redemption within the Circle of Election* (Caernarfon, 1819), in which there are some 'mighty flounderings'. In it Christmas Evans unjustly accuses Jones of Arminianism and of using 'angry, unchristian and immoral' language. He defends his former work against Jones's objections, though his views are not as rigid. He admits 'that he has abandoned the *commercial* theory of the atonement to a great extent and virtually holds that there was sufficient value and worth in the death of Christ for all'.

Thomas Jones, who was expecting the booklet on which he had commented, regarded Christmas Evans's turnaround 'as a breaking of a pledged word'. In retaliation he 'published a very hurtful and blasphemous poem about Christmas Evans and his "heretical" views. This proved to be a very bitter cup for the old warrior to drink.' Jones also defended himself in a letter dated 31 January 1820, in which he summarises their October discussions and denies treating his opponent unfairly. On 18 February of that year Christmas Evans replied in a 'simple, clear, moderate' letter that was probably composed by the Denbighshire pastors. Soon afterwards, in a letter from his own hand, he bitterly attacked Jones.

It is not known whether Thomas Jones would have replied to this attack, for the controversy was brought to a sad and unexpected end with his death on 16 June 1820, at the age of sixty-four. Christmas Evans was stunned. Years later the wounds of his battle with the Denbighshire minister were still raw, as he remarks: 'Oh what trouble was occasioned me by my controversy with Mr Jones of Denbigh! How it grieved me that he should have died and gone to heaven, as I fully believe he did, while we were engaged in that controversy! Certainly, I was not treated by him in a gentlemanly spirit; but if I could have foreseen the consequences, I should have allowed the storm to blow over, severe as it was, without saying one word. I now see much of my folly in other disputes, and, although unkindly dealt with, I ought to have borne it patiently rather than defend myself in an offensive manner. Let us not be too ready to rush into controversies, and when it is necessary for us to enter into them, let us do so in "the spirit of meekness".'

Both men were, to a degree, to blame—Thomas Jones for attacking his opponent with too much vigour, and Christmas Evans for taking an unscriptural, narrow and one-sided view of the work of Christ in his books; for becoming too involved in the personal side of the debate; for being unduly influenced, to his own detriment, by men less able than himself; and, while Jones maintained the infinite and illimitable sufficiency of Christ's work, for robustly attaching particularity to the atonement, and of course confining to that extent the sincere invitations of the gospel. Once Christmas Evans had understood that it was the infinite value of Christ's person rather than the depth of his agony or the weight of sin that decided the extent of the atonement, he became more guarded as to his dogmatic assertions and abandoned for good his mathematical concept of redemption.

'A sorrowing widower'

When Christmas Evans was nearing sixty he suffered the most painful and testing afflictions of his life. Undoubtedly one of the more pressing and heartfelt was the death of his beloved and excellent wife Catherine early on the morning of Wednesday, 22 October 1823, the day before their thirty-fourth wedding anniversary; 'and to no man could such a loss be a much greater calamity'. Catherine was fifty-seven years old. At the time of her death she was staying at the home of Robert Ambrose, minister of Bangor Baptist Church, awaiting medical treatment.

Catherine had been a perfect soul mate for her husband, lifting him up when the burdens of his ministry were set to overwhelm him; encouraging him with words of wisdom from the rich stores of her own faith; aiding him with the more practical side of ministerial life; offering support, with tenderness and intelligence, when the enemies of the gospel encamped around him. Throughout their married life she was content to live what must have been at times a lonely existence, without children, while her husband travelled throughout the Principality preaching the good news, but she was never heard to complain and was always ready to welcome her pilgrim home.

After her death, and while still in mourning, Christmas wrote a moving and graphic tribute to her in *Seren Gomer* under the title *A Sorrowing Widower and an Exile in the World*, a few extracts of which we give below: 'Her faculties were above the common order; she was diffident, but strong-minded. If she gave her view of a passage of Scripture, she never failed entirely, at least, of the mark. She had very elevated views of the sacrifice of Christ, which was her rock and strong tower. She was sharpsighted to discern men and things, and a little observation generally sufficed to enable her to form a pretty correct opinion. She speedily detected selfishness and conceit, however they might be attempted to be concealed under the guise of humility.

'She watched over her fellow-members in the church, and was sharp and earnest in her opposition to levity and sin. Her honesty was transparent;

and confidence in her was never abased. She was ever anxious to restore the straying, and bring back the prodigal. Her temper was excitable, but she readily forgave; to this there was but one exception during the forty years of her religious life:—in this case she had been grievously injured, and it required a long and arduous struggle to remove the agony, and to reinduce kindly feeling; but by earnest and protracted reflection and prayer, she was enabled, before she was called to eternity, to forgive the deep transgression, and to bury the very remembrance in the compassion and merits of the Redeemer.

'She never had robust health, but was a woman of good courage. She accompanied her husband on five of his journeys through the greater portion of Wales; and some in the depth of winter, through storms of rain and snow and hail, and over dangerous estuaries and ferries, with fortitude and cheerfulness. Her feelings were identified with the cause of Christ in her own land; its prosperity was her joy, and its reverses invariably produced anguish and bitterness of spirit.

'The last two years of her life were spent in much debility and pain; she had a complication of disorders, and was hastening to the grave. Great strength of spirit was given to her, and she submitted herself heartily to the divine will. The last night of her life, she frequently repeated a beautiful Welsh hymn; and, having three times cried out "*Lord Jesus, have mercy on me!*" she breathed forth her hopeful spirit into his hands.'

Christmas Evans was helped through his grief by the kindness of one of the island's young ministers, Hugh Williams, who preached the memorial sermon in Cildwrn Chapel on Saturday morning, 25 October. Catherine's mortal remains were buried in the small cemetery attached to the chapel.

The arduous labours and numerous duties that Christmas Evans had to perform began to affect his health, and his strength, under the strain, waned; yet, in the same year as his wife died, ignoring his own physical condition, he undertook a journey to South Wales in order to collect money for the chapel debts in Anglesey. On his journey he 'caught a violent cold, which settled in his eye', and for a time he lay on the brink of eternity. He received medical treatment at a hospital in Aberystwyth and was unable to preach for nine months. There seemed little chance of retaining the sight of his remaining eye, a constant 'thorn in the flesh' to him. Before his southward journey it had troubled him; in fact, for years it had grown steadily weaker, due to the exertions of travelling and preaching, and the lack of consideration he paid to his own physical welfare.

During this enforced sabbatical the friends at Aberystwyth paid him every possible attention. With their support and companionship his spirit retained its energy and strength, and he felt confident about returning to the pulpit, believing that God had a great work for him to undertake before he called him home, though many of his friends were convinced that his earthly course was about to finish. In due time he recovered and returned home, albeit in a much weakened state, only to become embroiled in a number of unhappy disputes with the churches under his charge. Over the next two years these contentions became more heated and personal, until he decided, with great sadness, to leave the island.

It was about this time, soon after his wife had died, that he was thrown into panic and fear by an insulting letter he received at a monthly meeting, 'at one of the contests with spiritual wickedness in high places', as he called it. It was from a 'brother' in the church, threatening him with civil prosecution on account of slander or a chapel debt or some such thing, for which he was deemed responsible, but of which he was entirely innocent. He was deeply disturbed by the threat of legal action because the honour of Christ's name was at stake, and with no human companion to confide in, he was brought to 'agony of grief'.

On his return home from the meeting he enjoyed 'fellowship with God during the whole journey of ten miles'. On arriving at his house, he thought to himself, 'This person and his relations threaten to cast me into a court of law—a place in which I have never seen. I will put him and them, first of all, into the high court of Jesus Christ, the fountain of law and authority.'

He then went upstairs to his room 'and poured forth my heart before the Redeemer, who has in his hands all authority and power'. The prayer he offered on this occasion is a beautiful example of the depth of communion he experienced with God, and the reverence and humble dependency with which he approached the throne of grace: 'O Blessed Lord! In thy merit I confide and trust to be heard. Lord, some of my brethren have run wild; and forgetting their duty and obligations to their father in the gospel, they threaten me with the law of the land. Weaken, I beseech thee, their designs in this. Disarm them, for I do not know the length of Satan's chain in this case, and in this unbrotherly attack. But thou canst shorten the chain as short as it may please thee.

'Lord, I anticipate them in point of law. They think of casting thine unworthy servant into the little courts here below; but I cast my cause into the High Court, in which thou, gracious Jesus, art the High Chancellor. Receive thou the cause of thine unworthy servant, and send him a writ, or a notice, immediately—sending into their conscience and summoning them to consider what they are doing. Oh, frighten them with a summons from thy court until they come and bow in contrition at thy feet; and take from their hands every revengeful weapon, and make them deliver up every gun of scandal and every sword of bitter words and every spear of slanderous expressions, and surrender them all at thy cross. Forgive them all their faults and clothe them with white robes, and give them oil for their heads, and the organ and the harp of ten strings to sing for the trampling of Satan under our feet by the God of peace.'

After 'about ten minutes in prayer', he was not wholly satisfied as he felt no inward assurance of acceptance or success. 'I went up again with a tender heart; I could not refrain from weeping with the joy of hope that the Lord was drawing near to me. After the seventh struggle I came down, fully believing that the Redeemer had taken my cause into his hands, and that he would arrange and manage for me. My countenance was cheerful as I came down the last time. I well remember the place—the little house adjoining the meeting house at Cildwrn, where I then resided—in which this struggle took place; I can call it Penuel. No weapon intended against me prospered and I had peace at once to my mind and in my (temporal) condition.'

He prayed frequently in this way 'for those who would injure me that they might be blessed, even as I have been blessed', and remained thankful to God for the furnaces of affliction in which he had been tried, 'and in which the spirit of prayer has been excited and exercised in me'. Needless to say, the threat of legal action was never executed, nor did he hear any more about the matter.

The battle rages

The Baptist meeting places in Anglesey at this time numbered about twenty, with many members attached to each one. There were twenty-eight ordained preachers in the various congregations, which, up to this point, constituted only one church of which Christmas Evans was the recognised head. These preachers, many of whom subsequently entered the regular ministry in Wales, England and America, were co-pastors with him *over all* the churches and had seen him, by the grace and power of God, turn a 'waste and howling wilderness' into a fertile plain, where the seed of the word, planted by his hand, grew and produced a crop. Several of them had been 'made free citizens of Mount Zion' through his instrumentality and consequently held 'their father and leader' in such high esteem 'that they would have him take the lead in all their deliberations and paid a due respect to his opinions on every subject'.

In his weakened state there proved to be too many preaching places for him to cover on his own, and he could not continue his pastoral visits as previously. He saw the wisdom of churches having their own ministers, so in a letter to the monthly meeting at Llanfair Mathafarn Eithaf in the summer of 1823, he 'encouraged and advised them to form themselves into [four] separate churches, or that every two or three stations should unite and call a minister'; and, as he wanted to retain a measure of control over these new bodies, he recommended ministers to them, although he regarded complete independency as the ultimate aim.

However, it appears there was a shortage of suitable men to meet the needs of the various branches, with many of the preachers bickering among themselves: 'We need men,' urged Christmas Evans in his letter, 'with more of the spirit of the ministry in them; men with no goal except to extend the kingdom of Christ.' Then in a postscript he advised them to 'change the Methodist plan or system, if you want to keep up with matters. It has been of benefit to us but it has served its purpose. We, by trying to work the whole farm, have failed to do justice to any part of it.'

According to Rhys Stephen, his intentions to 'divide the church' and his somewhat muddled and hesitant approach to the proposed changes did not meet with universal approval.

On 19 April 1825 William Morgan, from the Baptist Academy, Abergavenny, was ordained as the pastor of the church at Holyhead—the first on the island to appoint a permanent minister, in line with the larger Baptist churches of the mainland. Morgan was a fine preacher and unequalled on the island except by Christmas Evans, though he had a tendency to work too hard on his hearers' emotions. In 1839 he published a *Memoir* of Christmas Evans and gave the profits from the sales to Mary Evans, Christmas's second wife.

Some of the other branches, after witnessing the success of the church at Holyhead, also wanted to be independent and to step out from under Christmas Evans's 'absolute' authority, so they refused the ministers he recommended and accepted others whom he thought were too Arminian for Calvinistic churches. This defiance of his authority cast a black cloud of sorrow and distress over his mind. He thought their actions were deliberately provocative, and neither grateful to him nor beneficial to themselves, and with little hesitation or tact told them what he thought of their behaviour. Their reaction to his rebuke was one of indifference and even contempt, 'and he found himself, in certain parts of the island, superseded by his own children, or, what was more galling, by strangers'. As a result, a bitter party spirit arose.

One of the problems was that the church at Amlwch wanted to appoint the Fullerite Hugh Williams as their minister. This displeased a faction of the island's leaders, who feared that the cause would be ruined by Arminianism. Their views appear to have influenced Christmas Evans, who not only distanced himself from the lower Calvinism he had formerly embraced, but supported his old friend John Roberts, Pen-sarn, and not Hugh Williams, for the Amlwch pastorate. Inevitably, many who were outraged accused him of favouritism, and by June 1825, the situation was critical.

In the letter of the Anglesey Association of that year, Christmas Evans warned that 'church independence was threatening to get out of hand' and that 'God's judgement was about to fall on the rebellious'. In order to regain control, he 'advised the congregations to give precedence to the mother-church and its minister in all things, to refrain from seeking independence unless they had a lawful agreement with the mother-church before doing so, to choose only approved men to be ministers of these independent branches, and to ensure that no branch incorporates itself irregularly for personal ends rather than holy ones.'

The members of Amlwch were not prepared to submit to Christmas Evans's demands and some, angered by his rejection of Hugh Williams and his favouritism towards John Roberts, were 'guilty of blaspheming and disparaging the minister of the mother-church and by doing so belittled and weakened the discipline of the church throughout the country'. Others threatened to break away from his authority altogether, claim absolute independence and ordain Hugh Williams as their minister regardless of what the one-eyed preacher thought. Such an attitude infuriated Christmas Evans, who, after the monthly meeting at Capel Gwyn, 6 September 1825, excommunicated Hugh Williams, his father and four other members of the Amlwch connection 'for causing strife among the brethren'. Not surprisingly Christmas Evans was charged with dictatorship.

Hugh Williams reports what happened next: 'In that meeting, after the excommunication procedure, J. Roberts, Pen-sarn, announced that Christmas Evans would be preaching in Amlwch the following Sabbath. That night, the night of the service at Capel Newydd, quite a large number of Amlwch brethren gathered together. I yielded to their judgement; if they believed that my excommunication was according to rule, then I would submit and would be perfectly calm in my mind concerning the issue. They voted, as one, against my excommunication. Because there was great commotion in the town, it was decided that the wisest thing to do was to send word to Christmas Evans advising him that it would be better if he did not come to Amlwch that Sabbath in case he should bring more people with him and cause a riot to break out.

'The church decided to meet in a private house that Sabbath day, so we held our morning service at 2 o'clock in a house called Battws and the evening service in Palmer's house. Some time later many brethren from Denbighshire were called. A meeting was held at Pen-y-sarn and the unanimous decision was that Amlwch had been unfairly treated. This helped to soothe matters somewhat. But Christmas Evans and others expressed great dissatisfaction regarding the decision.'

From this time the Amlwch branch became an independent church, and, as its members had deliberately and publicly rebelled against Christmas Evans's authority, it signalled the beginning of the end of his reign on the island.

Meanwhile a problem had arisen at Holyhead, where the old church leaders clashed with William Morgan, accusing him, among other things, of 'Sandemanianism, spiritual pride and tyranny'. Morgan was furious at such outrageous charges, but instead of resorting to the monthly meeting to resolve the dispute, 'he was presumptuous enough to excommunicate them on the spot'. William Jones, one of the men expelled, held the keys to the chapel, and he decided, as an act of retribution, to lock the minister out of the building. At the monthly meeting at Brynsiencyn, 8 November 1825, it was decided not to blame Morgan, who admitted wrongdoing and promised not to act in such a way again, but to urge the excommunicated members to join another branch and to reopen the Holyhead church to the minister.

By early 1826 the dispute was so acrimonious that a delegation of four ministers from Denbighshire, at least one of whom was a Fullerite, was called upon to try to bring about a reconciliation between the factions. They met at Bodedern, but failed to bring the parties together. In fact, Christmas Evans's position was 'more precarious after this meeting than anyone could have imagined previously', which made him particularly sensitive to the arbiters. He regarded them as 'a real threat, not only to his own personal rule but to the good of the cause in general. That is how he interpreted a dream of his after the difficult meeting mentioned above. He saw four black bloodhounds attacking his mother and he had to defend her. The mother, of course, was the church in Anglesey, the dogs were the four ministers from Denbighshire.' As far as he was concerned the two reasons for the dissension were: 'the desire to enforce congregationalism in Anglesey and by so doing forfeiting church unity; and secondly, the supposedly unorthodox views of the younger preachers', which, he thought, would lead the churches 'headlong into Arminianism'.

Although his position as leader of the Anglesey church was threatened and the 'Arminian faction' growing in strength, Christmas Evans agreed to ordain Hugh Williams at Amlwch on the understanding that he would adhere to the 'old doctrines'. The service took place on 7 April 1826.

Instead of using the ordination service as an opportunity to restore unity, Christmas Evans wrote a letter to those who had been excommunicated at Holyhead, 'because I consider Wm. Morgan's behaviour towards you ungracious, rash, wrathful and irregular'. He was also angry with the men from Denbighshire for not standing against the 'young pretenders' in a more determined fashion, and, in a letter to John Roberts on 28 July 1826, accused them of undermining his authority and of being 'a great blessing to the inexperienced hotheads by their work in affirming the right of every church to call a minister, not to mention the danger of breaking the law of love with the sword of Independence. No one has the right to forbid anyone from consulting and seeking the advice and guidance of those who were fathers of the church in Anglesey.'

Christmas Evans was not deliberately contentious, nor disposed to maintain debates as to his rights, though he could be touchy and act rashly, and was often unwilling to yield to caprice and faction. Sometimes he was inconsistent and too severe in his judgements; on other occasions, when patience and tact were all that were necessary, he moved with undue haste and thereby aggravated a delicate situation. With his sensitive nature and powerful imagination, he tended to magnify the 'wounds of battle' so that 'the bite of a gnat became the cut of a sabre', and to react in a way that further rankled his opposers.

During the troubles in Anglesey there were occasions when he held onto his authority with an iron-like grip. Instead of allowing the individual congregations the freedom they desired, he insisted on their allegiance and submission, overreacted to their demands, and suffered personal rejection when they disagreed with him. He had served them faithfully with integrity for nearly forty years, and in return he thought he was entitled to their unwavering support. But with the wind of change on the island, he should have been more prepared to bend his will and compromise his ideals, keeping a clear conscience, rather than to resist the inevitable in a provocative manner.

On the other side, the Anglesey Baptists should have shown their father in Christ much greater respect and patience, treating his opinion, not with scorn, but with the deference it deserved. For them simply to 'throw out' his years of experience and to ignore the treasures of his wisdom as if they mattered little was an insult that weighed heavily on the aged warrior, who had fought so successfully on their behalf. But not satisfied with this insolence, 'some persons were unkind enough to attempt injuring my character by fabricating a falsehood upon me, which, though it was not criminal, yet it was a falsehood, and, as they say, had occurred (though it never in fact occurred) thirty-four years before'.

Leaves Anglesey

At times the censuring and strife among the Anglesey churches were severe and the wounds Christmas Evans bore so deep that he contemplated 'retiring, old as he was, from the field, the fragrance of which had proclaimed that the Lord had blessed him there'. Several older ministers, who were convinced that his usefulness on the island was over, were not slow in coming forward to voice their opinions, thus adding to his distress.

After he had left Anglesey he thought of himself when he remembered the fable about the old lion that had been king of the forest. 'Once every creature feared him and paid him homage. When he grew old and was unable to leave his den, all changed. The creatures gathered to despise him. Among the animals was Jack the Ass who turned his back to the lion and kicked him. That upset him more than all else.'

In his diary he expressed great wonder that 'I did not sink into the grave under the weight of sorrows that came upon me in my old age, together with an accumulation of trials of all kinds; but the Lord sustained me. There was in the midst of all a strong persuasion in my mind that there was yet much work for me to do for God in the world, as well as much to suffer, ere I died.' He felt sure that his ministry would be 'instrumental in bringing many sinners to God', a confidence that arose from 'my trust in God, and in the spirit of prayer that possessed me. I frequently arose above all my sorrows.' 'Nothing could preserve me,' he said, 'in cheerfulness and confidence under these afflictions but the faithfulness of Christ.'

With an assurance of future success, he continued to preach with great unction and was burdened, as ever, for the salvation of souls. 'If I only entered the pulpit,' he comments, 'I felt raised as it were to Paradise—above my afflictions—until I forgot my adversity; yea, I felt my mountain strong, my mind was in such a heavenly frame, and as anxious as ever for the conversion of sinners. The truth appeared to me in its power like a hammer in its strength. The doctrine dropped as sweet as honey, yea, sweeter than the honeycomb, and as comfortable as the best wine.'

He longed for unity among the ministers of the island and wished they would join him, according to the promise, 'If two of you agree to ask the *same thing*, it shall be given unto you of my Father which is in heaven'; for, he says, 'I had such confidence that then I should see prosperity attending the ministry, and that I should not die until I had finished my work'. He said to Richard Rowland, 'Brother, the doctrine, the confidence and strength which I feel, will make some persons dance with joy yet in some parts of Wales.' 'Yes, brother,' said he, with tears streaming down his face.

However, his desire for unity was not realised and it became increasingly difficult for him to exercise any meaningful influence in the monthly meetings and elsewhere. He could express his opinion and protest against the 'authoritarianism and independence of the young preachers', but he was in the minority and increasingly sidelined.

On 2 August 1826, the day of the monthly meeting in Capel Gwyn, the decisive 'battle' took place. Christmas Evans and 'his friends Richard Rowland, John Michael and William Roberts expressed their dissatisfaction with the events of the previous autumn, not only that the old pillars of the church, who had borne the burden and heat of the day with us for many years, had been expelled, but also that it had happened without William Morgan consulting the monthly meeting'. Then, rankled by the spirit of independence that was abroad, Christmas Evans said, 'We are not afraid of Amlwch, Llanrhyddlad or Holyhead because it is impossible to live with them; therefore we are going to set up our own house with no fear of the future. They have *broken the tie of church unity in Anglesey.*'

The following day, disillusioned and downcast, he wrote to William Jones and the others who had been expelled by William Morgan, and communicated his intention to leave the island, maybe for ever: 'I do not know for certain whether I shall ever see you again. Morgan's imperiousness,' he said, 'is one reason why I, C. Evans, am leaving the country.' For about a year he had wrestled with God in prayer, seeking guidance.

During those twelve prayerful months 'the visions of my head in the night seasons', as he called his dreams, appeared to confirm the leading of Divine Providence. Finally, after wavering between two opinions for quite some time, and believing he had found the Lord's will, he determined to leave Anglesey, a decision the islanders were soon to regret. In his own words, he says: 'Everything now contributed to remove me from Anglesey. The unbending disposition of those who were offended at me, and the ardour of my spirit, believing that there was work for me to do in some other field of the harvest of the Son of Man. I was much like Jacob, leaving his father and his mother, going with his staff only over Jordan; so was I, leaving the church. I had prayed, yea, I had strove with God for its prosperity and had laboured nearly forty years with it—now leaving it— possessing nothing of this world's goods, save the horse upon which I rode and a small amount of silver in my pocket; and scarcely could I say that these were mine.'

William Morgan, taking a retrospective view of the conflict, firmly believed that, whatever disagreements there were between the two parties, Christmas Evans's 'counsels ought to have been received with due acknowledgement of his age and experience, and that his reputation should have been energetically vindicated'. 'I am at this moment quite convinced,' he says, 'that more strenuous exertions should have been made to defend the character of the innocent; and I am also of opinion, and I say it with gratification, that had I seen things then as I do now, and possessed the same spirit, I should have endeavoured to bring the unoffending safely in my arms through the archers to a safe place, and would not have permitted Mr Evans's name to fall in the street without an advocate.'

He then paints a sad picture of the great preacher, who had worked so hard for the people of Anglesey, leaving his home, ostracized and rejected by his own spiritual children: 'It was an affecting sight to see the aged man, who had laboured so long and with such happy effects, leaving the sphere of his exertions under these circumstances; having laboured so much to pay for their meeting houses, having performed so many journeys to South Wales for their benefit, having served them so diligently in the island, and passed through so many dangers; now [some of the people] withheld their contributions, to avenge themselves on their own father in the gospel; others, professing to be friends, did little more; while he, like David, was obliged to leave his "city", not knowing whether he should ever return to see "the ark of God and his tabernacle" in Anglesey again. A dark cloud hung henceforth on the Baptists in the island.

'But God is good to his cause, and permits nothing to befall his people that is not for their good. He was merciful to Mr Evans, and protected him in his troubles; and we find room to hope in his mercy, that for the sake of Christ, and his name in the world, he will not permit the cloud to pour forth judgements on those who were misled, and whose arrows were bitter against his aged servant.'

There is no hiding the fact that Christmas Evans was deeply hurt by the trials he suffered in Anglesey and the unjust treatment meted out to him, but he was not a man to 'hold a grudge' or to look back more than occasionally with regret. Hence, as he meditated 'on the goodness of God towards me in Anglesey, both before going there and since I left', he could say with gratitude: 'Now in my old age, I see the work prospering wonderfully in my hand, so that there is room to think that I am a blessing to the church, and the church is such to me; whilst I might have been a burden to it, or rather a curse, by which she might have been induced to wish me laid in the earth, that I might no longer prevent the progress of the work. Thanks be to God, that it is not so! Though I deserve no better; yet I am in the land of mercy. This is unto me according to the manner of God unto his people.'

New life

After thirty-five industrious and productive years, during which the light of the gospel had spread its lustrous rays throughout 'the dark isle', Christmas Evans left the scene of his labours under a cloud of despondency. His health, exasperated by the troubles, had deteriorated rapidly and he was nearly blind; his robust constitution, usually vigorous and determined, was much enfeebled and reaping the effects of years of selfless exertion; and his legs, formerly so dependable and strong, were swelling painfully. In spirit he was downcast and, as many of his former friends had forsaken him, he felt lonely and insecure.

In July 1826, towards the end of the conflict in Anglesey, Christmas Evans was invited, on the recommendation of several respected ministers, to take charge of the Baptist Church at Caerphilly, Glamorganshire. On 28 July, he wrote to his friend John Roberts: 'I have received a call from the

Tonyfelin Chapel, Caerphilly. The smaller part on the left was the manse. The house on the right was the first meeting house.

church at Caerphilly and I am, after two Sundays, going there. It is time for Daniel to pray earnestly about the move to Babylon. If he can carry the old harps with him from Anglesey and sing the songs of Zion in Caerphilly to his satisfaction, then it is certain that the Daniel of Anglesey will go there to live and to die, according to his present thoughts. I am as popular in these communities as in any part of Wales; and the Lord has approved my ministry in these areas as much as anywhere in Wales.'

So, in the sixtieth year of his life, August 1826, and in failing health, he set out alone on a difficult and tedious journey of some two hundred miles to his new field of labour in the South. On his way from Llangefni to Brynsiencyn, and as he meditated on the affliction that had caused him so much grief, he 'felt such tenderness of heart, and that Christ's presence was so near me, that as the coldness of my nature dissolved, I could not refrain from breaking out in supplications and tears. The wrestling lasted for some hours.' His fears dissolved and faith triumphed, and, as he says, 'I had strength given me to entrust my ministry and myself to Jesus Christ with a confidence that raised me above all my troubles. I again entered into a covenant with God, which, however, I did not write.'

By the time he reached Caerphilly, a small village in a mountain valley, on 1 September, he was in a happy mood and thankful to God for his mercies. Before his arrival some of the residents of Caerphilly, who had heard the rumour of his decision to minister among them, dared not believe he would come, thinking that at the last moment his heart would fail him and move him to stay in his beloved Anglesey. His settlement in the area was an historical event in the region round about, and all denominations and conditions of people were caught up in the excitement, and with wonderment and gladness the report of his presence was propagated and received: 'CHRISTMAS EVANS IS COME!' 'Are you sure of it?' was the incredulous reply. 'Yes, quite sure of it; he preached at Caerphilly last Sunday. That I know from a friend who was there.'

He began his ministry at the Baptist Church in Caerphilly, without taking upon himself the pastoral care completely, in the same way as he had started in Anglesey, by calling the church together to pray that God would pour out his Spirit on them and prosper the preaching of the gospel. His aim was to secure through prayer the presence and blessing of God,

Plaque on a wall of Tonyfelin Chapel, Caerphilly

and subsequently the salvation of men, as is evident from his own remarks: 'I had heard that ministers and churches in America are favoured with great prosperity and powerful revivals, by continuing to seek them by prayer. I considered that the same spirit was with us; we agreed, therefore, under divine influence, to seek in the name of Jesus the outpouring of the Holy Ghost, with the word and ordinances, to render them efficient for the salvation of men and the glory of God. We succeeded, and received blessings in answer to prayer like that of which I had read as enjoyed by our brethren in America.'

On 20 November 1826, in a letter to David Richards, the first settled minister of the church at Caerphilly, he wrote enthusiastically, 'I have never been as comfortable as I am since I have been here. There is a great movement in this forest. We have received seven backsliders and thirty-six new converts. We have sixteen in the fellowship who are ready to be baptized and signs of many more. In the village of Caerphilly and the district of Bedwas, the breeze is blowing.'

A few days later he wrote to John Roberts and contrasted the 'happiness'

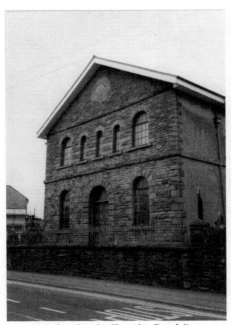

*Modern Baptist Chapel at Tonyfelin,
built in 1866*

of the Caerphilly church to have him as their pastor with the 'indifference' of the people of Anglesey to lose him. 'Praise the Lord, brother,' he said to Richards, on 15 April 1827, 'this final part of my difficult journey through the empty wilderness has been the most comfortable, entertaining and successful since the beginning at Lleyn.' Within two months of his arrival the regular congregation had risen to about a hundred and by the autumn of 1827 the membership numbered 160.

Unlike in Anglesey, where he had preached to different congregations, often using the same sermon several times, in Caerphilly he preached to only one congregation every Sunday and so needed a steady supply of new sermon material. He rose to this challenge, surprising many with the abundance of his resources, and making it clear, 'contrary to a pretty prevalent opinion, that his good preaching was not confined to a few good sermons, slowly prepared and often repeated; but that he was quite capable, from week to week, to get up discourses quite equal to his greatest and most celebrated single efforts'. Many of these sermons spread into other parts of South Wales. After the morning service it was common for members of the congregation to return home and discuss the sermon with their neighbours, so that by the end of the day throughout large areas of Glamorgan and Monmouth, Christmas Evans's morning sermon had been 'preached again' to many who had stayed at home.

They were also long remembered. Paxton Hood relates a conversation he had with an old lady, who, forty years after hearing Christmas Evans's

Plaque on the wall of modern chapel at Tonyfelin

sermons, said with tears, 'We used to reckon things as they happened by Christmas Evans's sermons. People used to say, "It must have happened then because that was the time when Christmas Evans preached *The Wedding Ring* or *The Seven Eyes*, or some other sermon" which had been quite a bookmark in the memory.'

Throughout the two years he remained at Caerphilly his preaching 'attained a power and an eminence it had never before reached, and it was crowned with lasting success'. Multitudes came to hear him, many travelling across the surrounding hills from all directions, and there were conversions and baptisms, not only in Caerphilly, where he had the pleasure and honour 'to examine about one hundred and forty candidates for baptism, and receive them by the right hand of Christian fellowship into the communion of the church', but in Bedwas and in churches as far away as Newport and Bridgend.

The young were especially affected by what they heard, and many notorious sinners submitted to Christ. Older people too, some of whom had lived a life of drunkenness, were so thoroughly transformed that publicans, angry at losing their most faithful customers, complained that since Christmas Evans's arrival in the area their 'intemperate profits' had been markedly reduced.

The people of Caerphilly had not experienced such a move of God for twenty-five years, and in response were filled with confidence and joy. Christmas Evans, in spite of years of prosperous preaching, had never seen such 'life in things'. 'There is no jumping or rejoicing,' he wrote in the letter to David Richards at the close of 1826, 'but much crying and singing. The chapel has become much too small during the last two months. Brethren from other churches gather in crowds on Sundays, particularly at the monthly services. The Sunday School is crowded out. I preach twice on Sundays and twice on weekdays, and in special services in the neighbourhood.' In a letter to the 'Gentlemen Managers of the Particular Baptist Fund in London' he remarks, 'I had never enjoyed such freedom and energy and success in any two years of forty-four of my ministry, as I have got at Caerphilly.'

Before the outpouring of God's Spirit and the influx of new converts described above, Christmas Evans had a remarkable dream, which he noted in his diary. This dream he believed to be of divine origin because of the blessing of God that attended his ministry at Caerphilly and because of the success of the gospel there: 'He thought he saw himself in a meeting-house very much like the one at Caerphilly, and hanging over and above the house there were many harps, wrapped in coverings of green. Then he said, "I will take down the harps of heaven here." In taking away the covering, what appeared but the Ark of the Covenant of the God of Israel standing opposite the table, and upon it was inscribed with golden letters in Hebrew,—JEHOVAH CABOD [JEHOVAH IS GLORIOUS]. Then he cried, "Brethren, thanks be to the Lord! Here he is come to us according to his promises, and to our prayers and expectations."'

It was under the place where he saw the harps that he welcomed the 140 new members, who, he says, had been tuned to the song of redemption.

'I want a wife'

Christmas Evans's salary at Caerphilly was £40 the first year and £48 the second year, which included a house, free from the usual rent and rates and situated under the same roof as the chapel, and adjacent to the chapel a small field (about half an acre) in which he kept his pony at a cost of £12 a year. He was also obliged to keep a maid, who was paid £10. He found it very difficult to make ends meet and would have run into debt had his salary not been supplemented by a small allowance of £10 from the Baptist Fund and the generosity of friends.

His health was generally good, although he broke a leg during his stay, but it mended well with little discomfort. Every month he preached around the neighbourhood. 'One great advantage of this house preaching,' he says, 'is that I do not go out to the cold air in perspiration, a great comfort to an old man.' In the same letter he makes the comment: 'I have no desire to return to Anglesey.'

Although Christmas Evans had 'no desire to return to Anglesey', it seems that his opponents on the island were sorry for the way they had treated him, and longed for him to return for the sake of the church. John Michael wrote to him in January 1828, saying, 'I went to Llangefni last Sunday. I was pleased to see their attitude. They have decided to hold a prayer meeting to implore the Lord to move your heart to come back to us. Oh that your mind could be inclined to come and visit your old comrades! I cannot imagine the joy that would be felt.' However, the memory of his departure was fresh in his mind and the wound still open.

Although he was settled in his accommodation, with a housekeeper, he mentioned to a friend that he would prefer a servant from the North as it seems his present housekeeper knew nothing about the mode of living to which he was accustomed. Upon discussing this change of personnel, it was suggested to him by his friends that he might marry again, and the name of a rich, noble woman was put forward along with the temptation of bettering 'his entire worldly circumstances by the alliance', and, because of her wealth, making himself 'pleasantly independent of churches and deacons and county associations'. When it was first suggested to him 'he seemed to think earnestly for a moment, then broke out, "Oh, oh! I tell you, brother, it is my firm opinion that I am never to have any property in the soil of this world until I have a grave. I shall then have my full share of it;" and he would talk no more on the subject.'

Some time later a friend visited him and found him in grave meditation, which he at length broke by saying, 'I want a wife, you see; I want a wife.'

'A wise thought, Mr Evans, if you can be well suited; but who is she to be?'

'They talk to me about Miss —, and tell me she has money; but it isn't money I want, but a wife.'

'Well, there is Mary, your old housekeeper; she knows more about your feelings and habits than any other person can do, and you know her. Will she suit you?'

'Aye, Mary—Mary, my old servant—aye, Mary is a good and faithful woman.'

He started to write to his former housekeeper Mary Jones, and in one of his letters proposed marriage. There is no record of her reply but letters passed between the couple for several weeks before he persuaded a neighbouring minister, Thomas Davies of Argoed, to travel to Anglesey— a round trip of nearly 400 miles!—in order to bring his faithful housekeeper to the South.

Davies set out with two saddled horses, telling all and sundry on the way that he was to return with a wife for Christmas Evans. On the journey north he preached at several chapels along the route, appearing in no hurry to reach his destination. Evidently Mary Jones took some persuading to leave Anglesey, but on Monday, 21 April 1828, she left Llangefni with her chaperone. At each stage of their journey they received welcome hospitality, and finally arrived at the chapel in Caerphilly on the following Thursday evening, just as Christmas Evans and his congregation were filing out of the prayer meeting.

On Monday 28 April, they were married by Rev. H. Williams in the presence of Richard Evans and John Williams in the parish of Eglwysilan, Glamorganshire, which is the same parish in which George Whitefield had married Elizabeth James of Abergavenny on 14 November 1741. The names of these great men are found in the parish register. Christmas Evans

Plaque in 'Lewis Arms', Tongwynlais
'In this room in 1827, Christmas Evans
preached on the occasion of the opening
of the Welsh Baptists in Tongwynlais.'

was sixty-one and Mary Jones, who signed her name with an 'X', was about thirty-five. The marriage was a very happy one and his new wife paid him the most untiring and affectionate attentions to the last moment of his life. 'Mrs Evans,' he remarked, 'has renewed her youth and is full of her first love—she sings as in the days of old. She talks of spiritual things all day long and never tires.' She survived her husband, and, apparently, in her old age and out of regard for the memory of Christmas Evans, C. H. Spurgeon secured for her a small allowance from an English Baptist fund.

Throughout his settlement at Caerphilly he was a caring and diligent pastor, who attended all the private meetings of the church, and endeavoured, by word and deed, to encourage the members of his congregation to walk in the ways of the Lord. He published a sermon, a biographical article and three essays with that aim in view. It is evident from his diary that the two years he stayed in Caerphilly were among the happiest of his life: 'I never spent a short time—about two years—in greater comfort; for the ark of God had appeared there.'

He had hoped to finish his course in that place, if it had been the will of Providence, but sadly problems arose. 'I had not my desire in that respect,' he says, 'owing to some things which brought no guilt upon my conscience, but certainly must have done so upon other persons. It is not prudent to notice them.'

The problems that he thought were 'not prudent to notice' centred on various disagreements between himself and some of his congregation. The deacons and members had for some years managed the affairs of the church, without the oversight of the pastor, Griffith Davies, who since his ordination in 1821 had lived in a neighbouring parish and at Cardiff. Davies was content to act as pastor, fulfilling his ministerial duties, without exercising the rights of a pastor to 'rule over' the church under his care. It was therefore the deacons who held authority in the church—an authority they were reluctant to hand over to their new pastor. Such a substitution of roles Christmas Evans could not tolerate.

With little or no direct controversy, he decided to leave. It was too late in life, so he thought, to change the habit of his mind to make it acceptable to the church, and there seemed little prospect of the leading members of the congregation compromising their position. He still loved many of them and desired their prosperity. 'May not our mistakes,' he said, 'be charged upon any of us in the day of judgement, but may we be graciously made to confess our faults on earth, where the fountain of grace and of pardon is opened.' No doubt the contentions that had caused him so much grief in Anglesey were resurrected in his mind, and rather than suffer the 'wounds of battle' again, he accepted a call, against the advice of some of his friends, from the Welsh Baptist Church in Cardiff.

Unhappy times

Christmas Evans had resided at Caerphilly for about two years when he was invited by the deacons of the Tabernacle Church, Cardiff, which was without a pastor, 'to come to them to try and raise the cause as it pleased God to be the case at Caerphilly'. After careful consideration and prayer for divine direction, and with no little anxiety pressing on his mind and exciting his feelings, he accepted the invitation, believing that it was God's will for him to labour, for some time at least, in that town.

Before removing to his new charge, which was only about eight miles from Caerphilly and in the same county, he entered into a new covenant with God, which he wrote out, dated and formally signed after his settlement in Cardiff. This covenant was the third he had made before God in the capacity of a Christian and a minister of the gospel, and it was found among some of his papers after his death.

Tabernacle, the Welsh Baptist Church, Cardiff

It was enacted on his return from the village of Tongwynlais in the vale of Taff, late one evening as he travelled over Caerphilly mountain, and while he was still uncertain as to the future. The spirit of prayer descended 'very copiously' on him. He wept for some hours and cried wholeheartedly to Jesus Christ for his blessings. 'I found at this time,' he comments, 'a particular nearness to Christ, as if he were close by me, and my mind was filled with strong confidence that he attended to my requests, for the sake of the merits of his own name.' The covenant is a heart-warming and challenging document.

After having entered into this covenant he went to Cardiff, 'heartily and unhesitatingly, like a merchant that should send his vessel to sea after it had been registered in the insurance office. I had nothing now to lose,' he comments, 'for I had given myself up to the possession of Jesus, the Mediator of the New Testament, for time and for eternity; and so I have had to abide here in the secret of his tabernacle for these nine months.'

He moved to Cardiff in September 1828, about 'nine months' after he had formulated the above covenant, and lived at 44 Caroline Street, just around the corner from the church. Many of his friends, who knew about the low spiritual state of the church there, caused partly by the conduct of his predecessor, who 'fell most horribly into immorality', shaking the church to its very foundation, did not regard it as likely to be a happy settlement.

Matters in the church were made worse by the fact that the disgraced pastor, who had been separated from the church because of his behaviour, remained in the town and attended the chapel, apparently without the slightest sense of shame for his conduct. Christmas Evans soon formed the opinion that he could find no marks of salvation in this man's life. In his letter to John Rowlands he says that 'without doubt [Pritchard] lived in sins such as adultery and drunkenness all the days of his ministry and was able to hide them by flattery, lies and craftiness'.

On 3 January 1829 he wrote to William Paxon, giving him details about the first three months of his Cardiff ministry, and enthused that the hearers were restored 'as numerous as ever'. During that time about twelve were baptised and five restored. As he was in the decline of life and suffering 'various debilities', he did not take upon himself the ministerial or pastoral care. Another minister was called to baptise, although he did administer the Lord's Supper himself.

He laboured with his usual energy and zeal for his master's sake, 'enjoying much and near communion with him, and daily walking in the light of his countenance', and longing for the 'Caerphilly experience'. He was greatly influenced by the revivals in America and Wales that occurred in 1828, and the Baptists and Congregationalists throughout England set aside Good Friday of that year as a day of prayer and fasting in all the churches to implore God to pour out his Spirit in like manner on them and on all parts of the world; and the following year the churches in England and Wales, including the Baptists at Cardiff, observed 17 April for a similar purpose.

Ten days later, from the prayer in his diary, it is obvious that he was experiencing various 'impediments and discouragements' in the church at Cardiff that were obstacles to religious progress, and harmful to his own walk with God, causing him more than a little distress. As with all things, he laid it before the Lord: 'Let things be ordered, O Lord, that they may not be impediments and discouragements unto me, and a hindrance to the progress of religion. O interpose between me and these obstacles, O Lord, that I may have no occasion to dispute with any, and so embitter my spirit! Thy power is infinite and thy wisdom is infallible. Stand thou between me and all contention that no ill effects come upon me. I flee to hide myself under the shadow of thy wings. Permit nothing to blunt the edge of

44 Caroline Street, Cardiff, where Christmas Evans lived

my talents, my zeal or my success—nor corrupt the church. Grant me this for the sake of thine infinitely precious blood. Set thy name to this request in the court of heaven, and let Satan's party grow weaker and weaker, and the cause of truth and righteousness become like the house of David, and the house of David like the angel of the Lord.'

The causes of offence within the church troubled him and it was not long before he felt uneasy. It seems that the church, as at Caerphilly, did not want to be ruled by any one individual, who would have the right to exercise the authority entrusted to him. So when Christmas Evans, a man used to taking the leading role, intervened to stop various old customs, great opposition arose.

To add fuel to the smouldering fire of discontent and misunderstanding Christmas Evans's view of church government was at odds with that of some members of his congregation. He was decidedly in favour of Independency, but was aware, particularly after his Anglesey experience, that it could 'be carried to too great a length, and become an unscriptural inundation, sweeping all away by the force of its current, and so prove extremely dangerous among Baptists and Independents'. He endeavoured to take a moderate view, with the authority of the elder or pastor kept in check, in the hope of avoiding the extremes that could arise. He was alert to the dangers of allowing too much power to the deacons, who were often ready to usurp authority.

The unpleasant differences of opinion and contentions that existed for some time in the church caused him much grief and sorrow, and drove him to cry out earnestly to God. Eventually, after further wranglings, he separated from the church with feelings of animosity, and several of the best and most faithful hearers, some of whom were leading men in the town, left with him and never returned. In spite of these troubles and disagreements, he could still say that 'there were many persons in the church at Cardiff, the most excellent I ever knew in any church that I had been'.

There is little doubt that there was a considerable abatement of power in his preaching at Cardiff, especially in comparison with his Caerphilly triumphs, which was partly due to his age and partly because of the constant wranglings in his church.

There were notable exceptions, however, especially on his travels. In 1829 a new English Chapel was opened in Charles Street, Newport, and Christmas Evans, along with Robert Hall, was invited to preach. Hall preached in English in the morning and evening, and Christmas Evans in Welsh in the afternoon. The former was 'overwhelming in the morning. The atmosphere was electrical, and the silence so intense it was as if no one breathed.'

In the afternoon Christmas Evans, who only had the text and main headings of his sermon in English before him, was 'at his mightiest'. Many shouted, 'Amen! Amen!', and Robert Hall, who sat in front of the preacher, with a burst of emotion cried, 'Glory be to God!' as the tears trickled down his cheeks.

After the service Hall followed Christmas Evans into the vestry, thanked him and, placing his hand on his head, exclaimed, 'May Jehovah bless you.' He then took Christmas Evans's 'hand in both of his and, looking straight into his eagle eye and bidding farewell, he left'. 'That service was spoken of for half a century afterwards as one of the greatest ever held in Monmouthshire and as one when Christmas Evans was par excellence the greatest preacher of his day.'

An important decision

Christmas Evans was eminently a man of deep devotion, who never undertook a new enterprise without earnestly seeking God's counsel. The slander he had endured during his long life, the troubles in the churches he had pastored, personal afflictions, coupled with extreme poverty, all tended to move him to approach the throne of grace on bended knees. He considered himself entitled, through Christ, to all the blessings of the gospel and to the immediate presence of God.

During his ministry at Cardiff he withdrew more and more from public gaze to fellowship with God, sometimes enjoying whole days and part of the night in secret and fervent prayer. His usual practice was to retire to his room for devotion several times a day—up to twelve times a day occasionally—and he frequently rose at midnight to converse with God. This prayer life was the foundation of all his work and the reason behind his success—a success that is amply borne out by the fact that, although his preaching powers declined during his troubled Cardiff pastorate, eighty members were added to the church under his ministry in the space of two and a half years.

However, in spite of his most vigorous and prayer-filled efforts, he failed to introduce better order into the church at Cardiff, which caused him increasing sorrow. So at sixty-five years of age and in a poor state of health, he felt obliged, 'through the intrigue of a faction, to retire from the two stations he occupied in South Wales, where his labours had been so signally blessed for the conversion of sinners'. God, he believed, had another field of labour in which he could sow the seed of the Word.

With that conviction, he gave himself entirely to the Lord, along with his wife, family, friends and assistants in the work of the gospel; and committed into his Father's wise and just care the troublemakers in the church: 'I have given my soul anew to Christ: my body, my talents, my influence in preaching; my name, my character as a man, as a Christian and as a preacher of the gospel; my time and the remnant of my opportunities; my success, my peace and comfort as a Christian and a minister. I have resigned all afresh into the hands of Christ. I have commended to his care also my wife and all the circumstances of my family and my friends and assistants in the work of the Lord, for whom I pray earnestly that they may be blessed.

'I committed to God also those who obstruct the progress of the cause here, and disturb the unity and brotherly love of the church. Let Christ, whose the church is, and let not me, remove every obstacle, either by changing and melting in the love of the gospel, or taking them somewhere else, where they shall not be a curse and an impediment to the cause—and by the means that shall seem fit in his sight.'

Towards the end of his stay at Cardiff, when he was assailed with conflicts from within and without, he wrote a letter to the editor of the *Welsh Baptist Magazine* (*Y Greal*), in which he views himself as an old general still on the field of battle. He looks back, with a touch of bitterness, over his long and eventful life, as well as forward to further usefulness, perhaps in another part of Wales. It is interesting to note that at this time he had received 'an earnest invitation to return to Llangefni in Anglesey': 'I am getting old and fast hastening to the side of the river. It is not easy for you as a young man to enter into the feelings of one who will soon bid farewell to all the tedious ways of the valley of life. They prefer their plans to his after all, and he is pained to witness their ignorance, perversity and presumption, especially as with their plans they have never achieved a single exploit. I have lived to see all this coming, without fail, to pass.

'It appears to me only as yesterday when I first went into Anglesey, my wife with me, on a day of unusual frost and snow. I remember the battles which I fought there; the powder and the fiery bolts of prayers and sermons; the sword, the bow and the arrow, the shield and the buckler, on the fields of Brynsiencyn, Llangefni, etc; the prisoners of war that were taken, and the arms and ammunition of the enemy that fell into the hands of the army of Emmanuel.

'Since I resigned the command in Anglesey, I have been looking out for fields which most required an old field-marshal, who knows how, through God, to handle as of old the sword and the bow. I took some part in the wars at Caerphilly, and by the mighty arm of the God of Jacob, some hundred and forty prisoners of war were led captive under the banner of

Emmanuel, and they were enlisted in his army in the course of a two years' campaign, as vigorous as any I ever saw.

'After that, the old field-marshal went to Cardiff, where the army was in the greatest danger, its leader having been shot down by great Diabolus. The divine power upon which the old field-marshal relies, took here again some scores of prisoners of war, and I trust they will be sustained in the new army to the end. My plan, since leaving Anglesey, where I was for nearly forty years, is to go to those places where there is required an old reaper, an old mower, as well as an old warrior; and to go on cheerfully as long as the army and the sub-officers submit to the king's laws, and do not frown upon me and "turn into their own ways" instead of listening to their superior.

'Since this is my plan, it need not surprise you to learn that I have taken the command in some other part of the land of Emmanuel. I don't know where I may end my days, but my prayer is that the Lord may give me some work to do while I am here, strength and peace to do it, and the help of Aaron and Hur to hold up my hands, by defending my person and my doctrine.

'I have received an earnest invitation to return to Llangefni in Anglesey, but I don't feel inclined as yet to go.'

His faithful friend, Daniel Jones, invited him to attend the Welsh Baptist Association in Liverpool, held during Easter 1832, and where he had been many times before. With the opportunity of consulting his ministerial brethren about his future, he gladly accepted. His appearance there delighted the members of the Association, who offered him every honour and comfort, and received him as one brought back from the dead. 'The energy that accompanied his preaching was astonishing; scores were stirred up to a concern for their souls, and life and animation appeared in the whole congregation.' Hundreds of others wept for joy to see him again in their pulpits.

During his stay the brethren, in order to discuss with him a destination and to advise him upon his future course, convened a special meeting. A group of ministers urged him to resettle in Anglesey, but those who pointed to Caernarfon, where the cause of Christ was low and the members of the church financially poor, outnumbered them. Christmas Evans was eager to return to the North, the home of his wife and the place where he had been so mightily used of God. By this time the enmity that had existed between him and the men of Anglesey had all but disappeared.

His desire to return to the North delighted the members, as they were deeply concerned about the Baptist cause in that part of the Principality. 'The spirit of prayer fell upon all present, and many a hearty petition was offered up to God that he might bless him there, and make him a blessing.'

His brethren, both Welsh and English, assured him that every effort would be made to secure a comfortable settlement, with all the necessities of life provided for him. Two of his friends in Liverpool, William Rushton and his son, supplied him with a small gig in which he journeyed north with his wife. His old horse, Jack, who was over twenty years old and had been his travelling companion when he had left Anglesey six years before, drew the gig.

He returned south in order to dispose of his furniture and make final arrangements for the move. After his last Sunday in Cardiff, which in a letter to a friend he called 'the ides of March', and his farewell sermon *The Death of Old Caesar in the Capitol,* he set out with his wife in the gig to Caernarfon, arriving there, with much trepidation, on a Friday evening in midsummer 1832.

Back in the North

Christmas Evans's arrival at Caernarfon was greeted with delight across the north of Wales and produced quite a sensation in the town. He was well known to most of the religious people there, having preached to them on many occasions during his ministry in Anglesey, and had proved to be very popular.

On the first Sunday after his arrival he preached at half past four in the afternoon in order to accommodate members from other places of worship. The chapel was crowded with expectant hearers, and many more gathered outside, so he positioned himself by the window and preached his sermon from that vantage point. For some time large congregations followed his ministry, on Sundays and during the week, but 'owing to the Baptists being few in number, and the effects of their former disordered state still remaining', and because in the main his hearers were members of other churches, when curiosity had been satisfied, they returned to their own spiritual homes.

At the end of his first year at Caernarfon the prospects of the church appeared more favourable, and he thanked God for the progress that had been achieved and the grace given to him. 'Many things are better than they were a year ago,' he observed. 'All things here were like a waste howling wilderness, yea, the dwellings of dragons, where they made their nest night and day. I do not know what the Lord may be pleased to accomplish here yet, "to the praise and glory of his grace". The sin of drunkenness, and the spirit of contention, were the two most dangerous monsters I met with in this town.'

Christmas Evans's popularity was never greater than during the last few years of his life, when he experienced renewed liberty and power in the pulpit, both in public prayer on behalf of small churches and other ministers, and in preaching. It is said, in answer to his petitions, 'that the spirit of prayer was never experienced so largely in all the churches and by all the ministers, excepting once, which was before the great revival in Anglesey'.

Some of the fruit of his preaching labours he never realised, as it was not

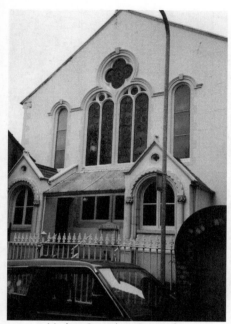

Modern Caersalem, Caernarfon

until after his death that several people declared him, under God, to have been the means of their conversion. His descriptive powers, which had always been forceful and impressive, continued to improve with age and his friends noticed how animated his talents remained—the cause of which he attributed to 'the peculiar goodness of God to him, who appoints one thing over against the other; the sweet against the bitter, and the cheerful against the sorrowful, that a balance counterpoise might be preserved'.

In July 1832, he attended the Anglesey Association that was held at Llangefni in a field very near to his old home, Cildwrn cottage. The announcement of his visit, after an absence of six years, created unprecedented rejoicing and anticipation, 'and it was thought that there were present on that occasion about two thousand persons more than usual, who had come expressly to hear him'. The people, who received him as one back from the dead, expected him to be frail in body and less animated than they remembered, but to their surprise and delight his appearance and preaching were full of vitality and vigour. As soon as he stepped onto the platform they were heard to remark: 'He does not seem at all older' and 'He looks more like a man of forty-five than of sixty-five.' He preached at ten o'clock in the morning with great fervour and effect from the text: 'And so will I go in unto the King, which is not according to the law; and if I perish, I perish.'

'His introduction was brief, as usual, and there was, it is thought, a visible effort to restrain and husband his emotions and energies through the less congenial task of statement and elucidation, which he was glad to

Inside Caersalem

get over as soon as possible, until his subject admitted of the full play and revel of his fancy, when he poured forth a stream of inspired imagery worthy of his mightiest days. The whole assembly yielded to the sway of his eloquence. Towards the close, he referred to his own past in Anglesey, to well-known preachers who had "entered into rest", and to the probability that "they should see his face no more".'

The older members of the churches in Anglesey, who could remember the religious state of the island before Christmas Evans's arrival, the changes for good he had instituted, and the resurrection of their own Association to great prominence, were overcome with feelings of joy to see the old preacher again and their love for him was renewed. This acceptance in the place of past trials was to Christmas Evans an answer to prayer, for 'he had earnestly besought his Lord that he might not be humbled in the presence of his former charge, and that the field of former achievement might not be the scene of weakness and confusion'.

Christmas Evans preached at the anniversaries of the Bible and Missionary Societies in Caernarfon, where his addresses met with great approval. He had always been a keen supporter of the Bible Society and willing to promote the cause of missions, often travelling to Bristol and London to enthuse support and declaring to all and sundry his vision of the ever-widening triumph of the gospel. It is said that Christmas Evans did more for the renaissance of missionary work and the birth of modern missions than anyone else in Wales, pleading with the churches and his fellow ministers to support the proclamation of the gospel in the newly discovered countries in East and West and 'for bigger visions and wider horizons'.

As has been mentioned the 'sin of drunkenness' was rife in Caernarfon. Christmas Evans, for most of his life, was far from being a teetotaller. In fact, 'word had spread abroad that he drank enough beer and spirits at a go to intoxicate six men', yet no one found any cause to accuse him of being drunk and disorderly. He himself admitted: 'I've been drinking a little for over half a century, without harming my body, my mind or my circumstances; nor have I disgraced the excellent name, through the great grace of heaven.'

However, the time had come, he thought, as an example to others and in regard for the weaker brother, to put away completely rum, gin, brandy and whisky, as well as beer and wine, and to throw himself, with his usual enthusiasm, into the temperance movement. He travelled to Liverpool, Manchester and Birmingham in support of its cause and his motto became: 'Touch not the liquid fire!'

In one crowded meeting he shared for the first time a dramatic dream, at the close of which, says a young observer, he looked up to the gallery and 'his one eye flashed as I have never seen any other eye flash in my life'. A fellow minister, Mr W— of A—, at the time could not lend his support to the temperance movement, and said initially that he would not be present to hear Christmas Evans, for he feared a personal reference to himself; 'yet such was the fascination that he could not stay away. He came to the meeting late and crept into the gallery, where the preacher's eye, which had long been searching for him, at length discovered him.'

Christmas Evans at once proceeded to say that the previous night he dreamt he was 'in Pandemonium, the council chamber of hell. How I *got there* I *know* not, but *there* I was. I had not been there long before I heard a thundering rap at the gates. "Beelzebub! Beelzebub! You must come to earth directly."

'"Why, what's the matter now?"

'"Oh! they are sending out missionaries to the heathen."

'"Are they? Bad news that. I'll be there presently." Beelzebub rose and hastened to the place of embarkation, where he saw the missionaries and their wives, and a few boxes of Bibles and tracts, but, on turning round, he saw rows of casks piled up and labelled gin, rum, brandy, etc. "That will do," said he, "there's no fear yet. The casks will do more harm than the boxes can do good." So saying, he stretched his wings and returned to his own place.

'After a time came another loud call, "Beelzebub!"

'"Yes," replied he.

'"They are forming Bible societies now."

'"Are they? Then I must go." He went and found two ladies going from house to house distributing the Word of God. "This will never do," said he, "but I will watch the result." The ladies visited an aged woman, who received a Bible with much reverence and many thanks. Beelzebub loitered about and when the ladies were gone, saw the old woman come to her door and look around to assure herself that she was unobserved. She then put on her bonnet, and with a small parcel under her apron hastened to a public house near, where she exchanged her Bible for a bottle of gin. "That will do," said Beelzebub with a grin, "no fear yet," and back he flew to his own place.

'Again a loud rap came and a more urgent call. "Beelzebub! You must come now or all is lost! They are forming teetotal societies."

'"Teetotal! What is that?"

'"To drink no intoxicating liquors."

'"Indeed! That is bad news. I must see to that." He did, but soon went back again to satisfy the anxious inquiries of his legions, who were all on the *qui vive* about the matter. "Don't be alarmed," said he. "It is an awkward affair, I know, but it won't spread much yet, for *all the parsons* are with us, and Mr W— of A—" (here the preacher's eye glanced like lightning at him) "is at the head of them."

'"But I won't be at the head of them any longer," cried Mr W—; and

Pulpit inside Caersalem,
with Christmas Evans's portrait

Christmas Evans's actual
pulpit at Caersalem, Caernarfon

immediately walking down out of the gallery, he entered the table pew and signed the pledge.'

During his Caernarfon pastorate he determined to look back over fifty years of ministering the gospel with thankfulness to God for his mercies and providential care. 'I had in the midst of all, great cause for thankfulness that the Lord had replenished my spiritual store and stock of thought to some considerable degree. I observe, with wonder, how my poverty contributed to my more general usefulness; for on that account I was obliged to travel very considerably, when otherwise there would have been no necessity.'

He also penned in his diary the following reflections: 'I have been thinking of the great goodness of the Lord unto me throughout my unworthy ministry, and now, in my old age, I see the work prospering wonderfully in my hand, so that there is reason to think that I am in some degree a blessing to the church, when I might have been a burden to it, or rather a curse, by which she might have been induced to wish me laid in the earth, that I might no longer prevent the progress of the work. Thanks be to God, that it is not so! Though I deserve no better; yet I am in the land of mercy. This is unto me according to the manner of God unto his people.'

Although Christmas Evans was still very much a 'blessing to the church', his earthly course was quickly drawing to a close.

Plaque on Christmas Evans's pulpit at Caersalem, Caernarfon

His last journey

It appears from a letter that Christmas Evans wrote to the 'ministers and members of the Baptist churches in Wales', probably sometime in 1836, that he had determined, much to his disappointment, never to 'attempt visiting my dear brethren in South Wales any more'. He had left home the previous year with the intention of touring the South, but his strength had failed him and he was obliged to return home.

The following year (1836) he tried again, but was 'afflicted with a severe disorder that affected my intellectual powers for a season'. With no prospects of future travel he sold his little gig and so lived, in his own words, 'like a bird shut up in the cage of old age, to labour almost if not altogether in one place'.

However, after he had resided in Caernarfon for nearly five years, the Baptist Church under his charge received notice to pay the outstanding debt of £300 on its meeting house. In order to meet this debt, he was entreated by the ministers at the Liverpool Association, Easter 1837, to embark, if he could, on a preaching tour through North and South Wales.

The following year, on 28 April, in compliance with their wishes, and in spite of his own feeble state and 'nearness to eternity', he set off, presumably in a borrowed gig, with characteristic ardour, on what would be his final journey through the Principality. His wife and a young preacher friend, John Hughes of Ruthin, one of his converts, who would serve as an assistant, accompanied him. Before he set out he penned in his book of last appointments the following prayer: 'O Lord, grant me my desire on this journey, for thy name's sake. My first petition: comfort in Christ, the comfort of love, the *bowels* of love and mercy in the denomination, the fellowship of the Spirit. Amen. The second petition: that the sermons I have prepared may increase in their ministration, like the five loaves and the two fishes. Amen. C. E.'

He also wrote in the same month (April 1838) a moving circular, stating the object and importance of his journey, and addressed by him to several ministers and through them to their congregations. 'The term of the lease of life has expired in my case, even threescore and ten years, and I am very much afflicted. I have purposed to sacrifice myself to this object, though I am afraid I shall die on the journey; and I fear I shall not succeed in my errand for Christ. We have no source to which we can now repair, but our own denomination in Wales, and brethren and friends from other communities that may sympathise with us.

'Oh, brethren, pray with me for protection on the journey—for strength and health this once, on occasion of my bidding farewell to you all—pray for the light of the Lord's countenance upon me in preaching; pray for his own glory and that his key may open the hearts of the people to contribute towards his cause in its present exigency.

'Oh help us, brethren—when you see the old brother, after having been fifty-three years in the ministry, now, instead of being in the grave with his colleagues, or resting at home with three of them who are yet alive—when you see him coming, with the furrows of death in his countenance, the flowers of the grave on his head, and his whole constitution gradually dissolving; having laboured fifty years in the ministry in the Baptist denomination. He comes to you with hundreds of prayers, bubbling, as it were, from the fountain of his heart, and with a mixture of fear and confidence.

'Oh, do not frown upon him!—he is afraid of your frowns. Smile upon him by contributing to his case this once for all. If you frown upon me, ministers and deacons, by intimating an irregular case, I am afraid I shall sink into the grave before returning home. This is my last sacrifice for the Redeemer's cause.'

His request was granted and everywhere he went he was cordially and joyfully welcomed, receiving generous donations of money towards the debt. He was very popular at this time, perhaps more so than at any other time, and wherever he preached large crowds assembled from an early hour to hear him; so much so that on many occasions multitudes remained outside the chapels, unable to gain admittance because of the throng.

He had arranged to travel until the end of September, going through Llanelli, Felin-foel, Carmarthen, through Pembrokeshire to Cardigan, and then back via Machynlleth, aiming to arrive home before the winter, but the Lord had determined otherwise.

On 6 June he reached Argoed in Monmouthshire in time for the

Association and preached at ten o'clock on the second day with great energy and powerful effect. This was his final associational sermon. 'Perhaps no sermon that Mr Evans ever preached evinced more vigour of intellect, more power and splendour of genius than this; and seldom, if ever, had he more perfect command over the feelings of an audience.'

Having enjoyed the blessing of God at this meeting Christmas Evans purposed to attend the Glamorganshire Association which was to be held at Pontypridd, but his frail constitution would not allow it, and a few days later he was laid up for a week at Tredegar in the house of Thomas Griffiths, a faithful Baptist. Griffiths, along with his son-in-law William James and John Roberts, showed him extraordinary kindness and did all in their power to relieve his suffering.

He was in good spirits, delighting to converse on spiritual things, and his humour was as sharp as ever. On one of the days, feeling somewhat stronger, he had gone downstairs and James was helping him back up. He had only managed a few steps when he turned to his assistant and said, 'Mr James, I daresay if I believed the French were behind me with their bayonets, I should find myself able to get upstairs without your aid.' At this he removed his arm from James's shoulder and ran up the stairs, laughing heartily at the feat!

After recovering his strength he continued on his journey to Caerphilly, where the main street was lined with people enthusiastically welcoming him back. He preached in his old church, and those who had formerly resisted his ministrations were pleased at his return, much to his surprise. On the way across Caerphilly mountain the carriage stopped at the place where he had made his covenant with God. He then moved on to Cardiff, where his old friends warmly received him. In both Caerphilly and Cardiff 'he saw that many of the old obstacles in the way of his former usefulness were now removed, and the evils which then existed less perceptible had appeared more generally visible, so that the good had become more commendable by the contrast'.

He proceeded to Cowbridge, Bridgend and Neath before arriving, with his wife and companion John Hughes, at Swansea on Saturday afternoon, 14 July. He was the guest of the celebrated blind preacher Daniel Davies.

'Wheel about, coachman, and drive on'

Christmas Evans preached at Bethesda, the Welsh Baptist church in Swansea, at ten o'clock on the Lord's Day from 'For I am not ashamed of the gospel of Jesus Christ', and again in the same place at six in the evening on *The Prodigal Son*. Both sermons were delivered with 'as much power and vigour as ever; his ideas and illustrations rising to the highest point, while he was exhibiting and commending the salvation of Christ to his numerous audience'. Daniel Davies comments that during his sermon on *The Prodigal Son* 'the large congregation was so completely in his hand that he could discuss the subject in any way he chose, and he returned to his lodging humming away, the usual sign that he was pleased'.

Mount Pleasant Baptist Church, Swansea

Inside Mount Pleasant Baptist Church

On Monday he appeared cheerful and conversed freely with all the friends who visited him, and in the afternoon he went out to tea with David Walters, 'a gentleman whom he had long known, and who was always proud to see and entertain him'. That evening he preached in English at Mount Pleasant Chapel from Luke 24:47. He was very feeble and tired, which worried both Daniel Davies and Rhys Stephen, the minister of Mount Pleasant, and somewhat awkward, as he was never truly comfortable speaking in English; nevertheless there were a few gleams of his usual brilliance that shone through to the congregation.

As he descended the pulpit steps very fatigued and sick in body he said in English quite distinctly so that a number present heard him, 'This is my last sermon', probably meaning it was his last in the town, but it proved to be the last of all. His wife Mary was very upset that he had been persuaded to preach as she knew it would be too much for him.

That night he was taken ill, with an attack of what was then thought to be erysipelas, but the doctor was not called as Mrs Evans thought it was one of his usual turns. Through the greater part of that night and the following day he was in a partial stupor and taking little notice of the many friends who called upon him. 'He was in the afternoon as a piece of wood, without the inclination or ability to stir, as his wife struggled to turn and treat him, for she would not allow anyone else to touch him.' She was adamant that a doctor should not be called, although she did promise Daniel Davies that if he was not better in a day, he could call for medical help. Christmas Evans was convinced he would recover, remarking in one of his more lucid moments: 'Don't think, dear Davies, that I'm going to die. I know that I am not going to die now, because there's an old pact between me and the Almighty that I will receive a sign from him at least a fortnight before I die, and I haven't received that sign yet.'

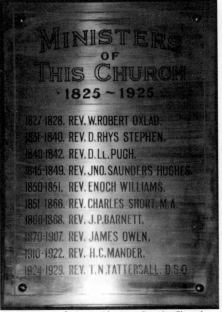

Ministers of Mount Pleasant Baptist Church

On Wednesday 'the powers of his mind seemed to be quite restored, and his body tolerably free from pain, but he complained of some difficulty of respiration, which gradually increased'. He rose about midday and walked for some time in the garden to try his strength, with a view of going to preach at Llanelli on Sunday. Many called to see how he was and he conversed with them cheerfully, feeling refreshed by their visits, but he still found it difficult to breathe, remarking to his friends that he had never experienced such symptoms before.

Towards evening he relapsed and it was suggested, because of his respiratory problems and a noise in his throat, that a doctor should be called. When the doctor arrived he asked him earnestly when he thought he might be able to resume his work, although 'he appeared', said his friend and companion Mr Hughes, 'as if something whispered to him that his earthly career was about to terminate, and that he was to expect in a very short time, the summons of his Lord and Judge'.

As if to confirm Hughes's opinion, Christmas Evans said to the doctor, 'If you are going to give me any medicine, sir, pray, whatever you give me, don't give me any opium; for if I am going to die, I wish to die with my senses about me, so as to have full control of my thoughts and expressions.' By this time the doctor, who had diagnosed a heart disease, knew there was nothing else he could do. He called Daniel Davies to one side and said, 'I am afraid it is quite useless to give him anything with a view of saving his life.'

Between one and two o'clock on Thursday morning Christmas Evans called his friends John Hughes and Daniel Davies, whom he thanked for the hospitality and kindness he and his wife had been shown. He talked about one of his dreams, in which he had seen himself approaching a great river which he thought he did not have to cross, so he turned back, believing it to be a sign that his work was not yet complete, although he admitted, 'I had not received a command to turn back from the bank of the river; so it has now become *wheel about*, and it is necessary to go through it, but thankfully, there is no danger. The High Priest is in sight, the land too is in sight for my eyes are focused on the shore yonder, and the sound of music reaches my ears from the house of my Father.'

Then, with a holy triumph that seemed to pervade his soul in the prospect of an eternity of glory, he said in Welsh, 'I am leaving you; for fifty-three years I have laboured in the sanctuary and my comfort and confidence on this solemn occasion are this, that I never laboured without blood in the vessel. Preach Christ to the people, my dear brethren. If you look upon me as I appear in my preaching, I am lost for ever; but look at me in Christ, I am in perfect bliss and am saved.' He then repeated in a clear voice a stanza from one of his favourite Welsh hymns, about the completeness of the righteousness of Christ to clothe the naked sinner and render him acceptable to God, and expressive of his firm trust in his redeemer.

About an hour later, he waved his hand and exclaimed in English, 'Wheel about, coachman, and drive on,' as if spying the chariot of fire from heaven. He turned over and without a struggle or a groan slipped into a state of unconsciousness. Mary thought he was sleeping as his breathing

Bethesda Baptist Chapel, Swansea

was so heavy, and she persuaded everyone to leave the room for a time so she could quietly care for him. 'After we'd listened carefully for two hours to the loud noise that came from his mouth, going now and again into the room,' Davies recalls, 'everything suddenly went silent, and though we hurried, we only just reached the side of his bed by his last breath. He gave only one sigh after we'd entered the room.'

Mary was asleep in the chair by his bed. His friends tried to rouse him, but it was too late. The chariot had come and taken him through the river to his eternal home. Thus, amidst the songs of angels, Christmas Evans died in the home of his friend Daniel Davies in Swansea at about four o'clock in the morning on 19 July 1838, in the seventy-second year of his age and after more than fifty years in the ministry. The Lord had hurried to his rescue, remembering the words of his servant's covenant: 'Leave me not long in affliction, nor to die suddenly, without bidding adieu to my brethren, and let me die in their sight, after a short illness. Let all things be ordered against the day of removing from one world to another, that there be no confusion nor disorder, but a quiet discharge in peace.'

Christmas Evans's grave and memorial in Bethesda graveyard

A deep sense of grief and loss gripped the hearts of thousands throughout the Principality, especially those in Anglesey who had known him so well and profited from his years of service. The funeral service, in which several ministers took part, was held on Monday 23 July, in Bethesda, the Welsh Baptist Chapel in Swansea. The news of his death had spread rapidly and a huge concourse of mourners, more than ever before for a funeral in Swansea, all anxious to pay their last respects to a man they revered and loved, and to whom hundreds had listened with joy only a few days before, gathered from near and far. It was remarked that 'so much sorrow was never before witnessed on an assemblage of people as at this funeral'. He was buried in the grounds attached to the chapel, with great honour and mourning, and according to Welsh custom.

'Having reached Bethesda meeting house, the Rev. John Saunders of Aberystwyth (Congregationalist) read a portion of the Bible and prayed; Rev. D. Rhys Stephen, of Mount Pleasant church, preached in English, and the Rev. Daniel Davies of Bethesda, in Welsh, and the Rev. David Roberts (Calvinistic Methodist) closed in

Christmas Evans's grave and memorial in Bethesda graveyard

Memorial of Christmas Evans and Thomas Rhys Davies

Memorial of Christmas Evans and Joseph Harris

prayer. At the grave the Rev. Joshua Watkins of Carmarthen, delivered an impressive oration; then the body of the great Christmas Evans was laid low, under the lock of the dark tomb, where his cheerful smile can no more be seen, and from whence his eloquent tongue can no more be heard, until the morning when the "Resurrection and the Life" shall call his ransomed home.'

So this great man and preacher, whom God equipped and used in such an extraordinary way, passed from the shores of this world to the eternal haven of rest. He is silent now and his voice, with its majestic tones, will never again thrill vast congregations or echo round the surrounding hills, but he must never be forgotten; for it is through men of his mould, who are wholly devoted to the service of Christ, that our Saviour ushers the lost into his kingdom of grace and light. As a soldier in the army of God he fought the good fight. He finished the course marked out for him and he kept the faith. Henceforth there is laid up for him a crown of righteousness, which the Lord, the righteous Judge, shall award him on that day; and not only to him, but to all who have longed for the appearance of Christ.

No ordinary person

When Christmas Evans started preaching he was bony and thin in the face and somewhat clumsy in his movements, but as he matured his face filled out, the traces of consumption that had at one time afflicted him disappeared, and his bearing became more refined. He was well-built and of a strong constitution, with 'a majestic appearance'. David Phillips, who was acquainted with him for some thirty years, describes him as nearly six feet tall. 'In his best days he was rather corpulent, but sometime before his death he grew much thinner, and was rather inclined to stoop in his shoulders. His countenance was broad and open, and his forehead large, calculated to strike the beholder with the idea of power and authority [his head was so large that his hats were either split to make them fit or made to measure]. His one eye was somewhat larger than common, and rather prominent.'

In addition to his rather striking physical appearance, he was known to be 'utterly regardless of his own health, ridiculously inattentive to his dress and to all his travelling arrangements'. Commenting on the medicines he tried, Brutus says: 'He took, no one knows how much, opium, bark, pellets, drops, patents and every concoction, and if he saw anyone taking medicinal drugs, he had to try them out himself. I never knew anyone with such a strong constitution, and if it were not for the fact that he was strong, he would doubtlessly have killed himself. He took enough opium once, at a go, to send three or more men into an eternal slumber; and he would take Peruvian Bark, Pills, Drops, etc. in such doses that you would not have given a halfpenny for his life; but they had no more effect on him than if they had been dropped into an elephant's bowels.'

When he took snuff, he often spilt it on his clothes and was unconcerned about brushing it off. 'No one had ever seen,' continues Brutus, 'either before or after, such a mess on any man's front as on Christmas Evans's front during his *snuffing fit*.' His clothes, it is said, were worn 'as if they had been thrown on by a pitchfork', and no matter how hard his wife and friends tried to rearrange them, within minutes they were untidy again.

It was not simply his outward peculiarities that made him an unforgettable character—it was the strength of his inner walk with God. Christmas Evans was a man who possessed the spirit of prayer to a remarkable degree. Once he said, without the slightest exaggeration or Pharisaical boastfulness, 'A thousand prayers bubble up from the fountain of my soul.' 'I never succeeded in anything for the good of others,' he remarked on another occasion, 'without making it a matter of prayer.' He had a devotional frame of mind that entered frequently and fervently into fellowship with God, which he considered to be the soul of religion. He perceived constancy in prayer to be 'as necessary to the spiritual life as breathing is to the natural one. Prayer has been to me a kind of friendly intercourse with heaven, when I have cast away my burdens and had grace in time of need.'

'Sometimes he would be elevated to such a pitch of importunity and holy boldness, and be carried away to such a degree, as to repeat the same petition several times. Once he did so *thirteen* times; and no less than *thirteen* sinners were converted to God at that time! When the last of that number had related his experience before the church, the deacon, who had counted the repetitions and been somewhat displeased, came forward and acknowledged his fault.'

Perhaps there were no occasions when the spirit of prayer fell on him more copiously than before the assault of some 'inward foe or external enmity'. Then Christ followed him with the sufficiency of his grace and gave him two things in particular: 'namely, some premonition (in a dream or otherwise) that a storm was approaching, and a spirit of prayer, with a renewed enjoyment of his presence, until I became a prince in the confidence that the Lord Jesus was in alliance with me, like Jacob when he met with Esau. No Esau succeeded against me; and the omen of victory, at all times, was the spirit of prayer.'

Along with being a 'wrestler with God', Christmas Evans was a gentle and humble man, whose conduct was characterised by a diffident and quiet spirit. 'His fervent piety, holy zeal and unblemished life, secured for him the respect of many warm-hearted Christians,' who recognised him as a 'holy man of God'. Brutus, in reference to his godliness, remarked that 'not only was Christmas Evans a wonderfully great man, but he was God's man'. He was especially careful to walk with circumspection before the world so as not to give the enemy of souls any opportunity to slander the name of Christ or to bring his cause into disrepute.

He endeavoured at all times to establish and maintain true discipline in himself and others, believing that the doctrine of Christ in the profession, and the spirit of Christ governing the heart and conduct, were reasons enough to support a well-ordered lifestyle. Persons of unbecoming deportment could expect nothing less than his strong disapproval, which occasioned him much trouble from some members of the churches where he ministered.

He was very zealous for the things of God and utterly sincere and honest in his dealings with others, never seeking an advantage by underhand or devious means. He thought that any departure from the truth, in word, behaviour or belief, was a disgrace both to the gospel and to a man's Christian character. At times he could be unsuspecting to a fault, and some crafty persons would treat his innocence with cruelty. Sometimes he was taken in by flattery or by an eloquent and persistent tale-bearer, but when he investigated the matter and discovered the truth, the injured person received his full protection and support to the disgrace of the slanderer.

His straightforward honesty is wonderfully borne out by the following well-known anecdote. He had employed a person to sell a horse for him at a fair and after a while he went out to see if the man had been successful. 'There was a stranger bargaining for the animal, and the contract was nearly completed. "Is this your horse, Mr Evans?" said the purchaser.

'"Certainly it is," he replied.

'"What is his age, sir?"

'"Twenty-three years."

'"But this man tells me he is only fifteen."

'"He is certainly twenty-three, for he has been with me these twenty years, and he was three years old when I bought him."

'"Is he safe-footed?"

'"Very far from that, I assure you, or I would not part from him, and he has never been put in a harness since I have had him either."

'"Please go into the house, Mr Evans," whispered the man whom he had employed to make the sale, "for I shall never dispose of the horse while you are present."

'The frank manner, however, in which Mr Evans told him all the truth, induced the dealer to make the purchase at a very handsome price; while he procured for Mr Evans a good name, which is better than gold.'

He often expressed the hope that, by the grace of God, he had overcome the corruptions of his heart, especially his natural disposition towards an angry, revengeful and unforgiving spirit. In this matter he was generally victorious, for although he suffered greatly from the accusations and behaviour of his opponents, he was usually ready to forgive them and to resist vindictiveness. He took more pleasure in pardoning the offender than in any apology offered.

He found it hard to resist any plea for help. 'Once a brother in Anglesey, together with his family, had been sick for some time, and in consequence was reduced to a very low state as to his circumstances. Mr Evans felt much for him, and relieved his distress to the utmost of his ability—even by giving him the *only* pound that at the time he possessed. His wife remonstrated with him for giving away the money, adding that they had none to buy food the following Saturday; to whom he replied, "Food will come to us yet through Providence from some quarter." The day before the market he received a letter from a friend in England, begging his acceptance of the enclosed *two pounds* for his own use. When he had read the letter he said to his wife—at the same time showing her the two pounds—"Catherine, I told thee that Providence would return the alms-pound, for it was a loan to the Lord."'

At times he was not always wise in what he said, being too impulsive for his own good in voicing an opinion. John Jenkins, with whom he often quarrelled, commented that he had never known anyone so great in godliness and yet so childish. During the troubles that led to his removal from Anglesey, when his position was threatened, he referred to the Denbighshire arbitrators as 'merely cabbage stumps', and spoke of Samuel Edwards, one of their number, as a 'horse-angel'. His contention with Edwards became very acrimonious. 'It is said that C. E. fainted during the dispute. They were both in the same room and Ellis Evans said that they came out very short of breath and their spirits amazingly tender, like two giants that had expended all their energy on each other.'

In conversation he was friendly and knowledgeable, and at ease in the company of different classes of society. 'If he had confidence in the persons present, he would be exceedingly agreeable and cheerful; he would listen attentively to every one that took part in the conversation, and offer pertinent remarks himself on the subject that engaged the attention of those present. If any officious person should advance anything impertinent, for the sake of showing himself, he would assume a gloomy aspect for a short time, but having silenced that individual, he would resume the conversation with fresh animation.'

Although he had no children of his own, he enjoyed the company of children and possessed a familiar and tender disposition towards them. He could easily and quite naturally turn aside from conversing on some profound and glorious topic with another minister of the gospel, who was left with a sense of wonder at the things he had heard from him, to a small child, take him on his knee, and impart to him a word or two about the Saviour's grace and love. 'He would use no silly fondling, as some foolishly do, but would give some advice, or instruction, or some little easy verse, suitable to the temper and the age of the child; and generally what he said in this manner would be remembered after he was gone.'

He was never vulgar or harsh in his conversation, but he did exercise a keen sense of humour, which delighted his companions. Once when crossing one of the Merioneth mountains on a midsummer's day, he accidentally met John Herring, a talented Baptist minister from Cardigan, who greeted him with the words, '*Dear me*, this is very wonderful, to see Christmas in the middle of summer.'

'Well,' he immediately replied, 'that is not more wonderful, that I know, than to see a live herring on the top of a mountain.'

On other occasions he used humour as a last resort, when reasonable arguments failed to achieve their objective, as in the case of a minister friend who was afraid of a French invasion. This good brother, who was also a tailor, expressed his concerns in the most doleful manner to Christmas Evans, who tried hard to comfort him by assuring him that God, not Bonaparte, ruled the universe.

When his words of consolation failed to lift the spirits of his friend, he adopted a completely different approach. 'I will tell you, brother, what you must do,' he said gravely, as if to address the sufferer with yet more serious counsel: 'When the French are about to land, you must fix your needle into one end of your yardstick, fasten the red sleeve that holds your needles in front of your hat, hang the thimble under your nose and tie your iron and sleeve board round your waist. When you hear that Boni has landed, whistle into the thimble to rouse the country; and when you meet the army, beat the sleeve board with the iron. When they see the red sleeve and hear the noise, Boni and his army will be terrified and flee. You must pursue them mercilessly with that needle protruding from your yardstick!'

As a minister he was not adept at theological debates, although, partly because of his prominent position in the Principality, he engaged in several controversies of the day, but more out of necessity than desire. His nature was too sensitive for the rigours of disagreement and often, in the heat of battle, he was wounded by criticism or abuse, making him wish that he had never entered the fray. He preferred to be applauded than slandered, and responded favourably to the approval of others.

In his early ministerial career he tended to be overly severe with those brethren who opposed him, though he never regarded them as unregenerate or in any way inferior to him, and too vigorous in the defence of his opinions. In his polemic writings there are occasions when he deals with his challengers offensively, even slanderously. Sometimes, in order to get the upper hand, he would try to confound his opponents; at other times, he would be too hasty in sharing his views, often without sufficient contemplation on the subject under discussion, and too skilful at colouring his arguments. He could, however, when the occasion demanded, be both reasonable in response and fiery in rebuke.

The principal danger in the conduct of his mind was the temptation to govern all his thoughts with what could be an unbridled imagination; 'and there, conjuring up forms and figures and modifications from his comparatively extensive and most observant and attentive reading, he framed worlds and states of things of his own', which did not always agree with reality or the doctrines of the Bible. At times he was too easily swayed by what he read, particularly if the author presented his arguments in a strong and brilliant style. The eloquence of the pen charmed and convinced him.

Finally, his friend Rhys Stephen highlights the two principal qualities of

Christmas Evans's life: namely, a 'heart swelling with love to God and man', and a determination not to live for himself but for Christ Jesus, before whom 'he was ever prostrate, ever devout'.

Communion plate and cup used by Christmas Evans when he was minister of Caersalem Baptist Church, Caernarfon (1832–1838). They are held in the Museum of Welsh Life, Cardiff.

An extraordinary preacher

No study of Christmas Evans would be complete without an examination of 'the man in the pulpit', who, 'for successful popular eloquence among his own people, ranks among the most remarkable preachers of his age'.

The message he preached was the old-fashioned gospel of 'Jesus Christ and him crucified', and his main themes were the fundamental truths of the Christian faith. He proclaimed the great salvation of God in a purely evangelical sense, all the time stressing the sufficiency of Christ for redemption and man's inability to earn by his own efforts the forgiveness of sins. He believed that 'Jesus Christ represented his people in his mediatorial capacity; that he fulfilled the engagements of the covenant on their behalf; that he sealed their redemption on the cross; that he arose as the firstfruits of their resurrection; that he is now in heaven interceding for them; and that ultimately he will be entitled to see the whole family of the redeemed in glory and happiness'. 'Christ,' he would say, 'is the whole of our salvation, our hope and our happiness.'

His aim in preaching was to arouse careless sinners out of their lethargy and to lead them to Christ. 'May these remarks,' he said at the end of one of his sermons, 'preserve you from despair under a sense of your guilt and wretchedness; drive you from all false refuges to the cross, with a penitent and grateful heart; induce you to trust, not in your own strength or wisdom or righteousness, but in the adorable name of Jesus; to live a life of faith in him, of love towards him, and of patient waiting for his mercy unto eternal salvation.'

However remote or obscure his text, he would soon lead his congregation up the hill of Calvary, and focus their minds on the cross. 'Now my hearers, let us go to Calvary,' he would say. 'What an amazing sight!' Once he cried, 'O Calvary! Calvary! How could I ever pass by without looking at you.' Arthur Jones of Bangor says of him, 'His great and vigorous soul was like a man who had been born and bred in the temple, taking a walk every day, for the benefit of his health, to the hill of Calvary, the garden of Joseph of Arimathea and Mount Olivet, till he grew up the most healthy young man that ever existed.'

Christmas Evans had not only understood these doctrines in an intellectual sense, enabling him to impart truth to his hearers, he had also been profoundly moved by them in his own heart. He had experienced for himself the deep things of the gospel, and his sermons, effectual and thrilling as they were, were an overflow of that experience. A preacher, he thought, rather than being just a dry and passive mouthpiece, should be filled to overflowing with his subject, overcome by it almost, and aroused by the influences of the Holy Spirit, so as to produce a meaningful and lasting impression on those who listen. His object was not only to enlighten the understanding, but to warm the heart that all should *feel* as well as see the glories of Christ.

Thus, when he stepped into the pulpit 'his soul was kindled and inflamed by the live coals from the altar. His words and thoughts became radiant with fire and metaphor; they flew forth rich, bright, glowing, like some rich metal in ethereal flame.' He was like the fiery volcano of 'Etna or Vesuvius, pouring the lava of his own eloquence in a torrent of liquid fire on the heads of his hearers, until their feelings kindled and burned with the intensest glow'. He spoke with the whirlwind and the storm, with words that broke rocks into pieces, his one eye flashing as his whole being was stirred to the depths by the truths he uttered. At times this 'glorious dramaturgical Boanerges', as he has been described, preached with such impassioned earnestness, being so full of the love and power of God, that he seemed quite overwhelmed with the greatness and magnitude of what he was saying, and trembled like an aspen leaf.

This passion, which cleared away everything before him, and the divine anointing, which made the truth shine so brilliantly, 'often rendered him superior to himself, clothed him with a superhuman energy, till he seemed a messenger from the other world. The man was lost in his theme. Art was swallowed up in the whirlpool of excited feeling. The audience were swept irresistibly along by the current of the discourse; acknowledging by tears and groans the preacher's hold upon their hearts; and sometimes losing all self-control, and bursting into the most extravagant expressions of wonder and delight.'

'At times, however, the noise of the greater part of the congregation was offensive to persons of refined taste; and sometimes he was under the necessity of retiring, leaving the field or the street where he had been preaching, full of people, some in the greatest agony of mind, crying out for mercy; others praying, others singing, and a great many jumping; while many spectators were gazing, some with great approbation, firmly believing that God was among them, that his arm was made bare in the conversion of sinners, and that nothing less than Almighty power could accomplish such mighty works.'

Throughout his ministry Christmas Evans was 'captivated and enraptured by the wondrous story', expressing it with an imagination of genius that thrilled his listeners. Imagination was the principal power of his soul, uniting and absorbing, and sometimes overshadowing all his other talents, bold in its course, prolific and adventurous in flight, gripping in magnetism. 'He was often illogical, but he had a gorgeous and excursive fancy which invested his sermons at times with a charm and a power that were wholly resistless.' Owen Thomas of Liverpool thought his imagination to be 'one of the most fruitful that ever belonged to a man'.

The brilliance of his imagination gave rise to comparisons with Milton and Johann Paul Richter, while its creativity, coupled with a copious vocabulary and flowing eloquence, earned him the title *The Golden-Mouthed Chrysostom of Wales*. Some, recognising that many of his sermons were sacred poems, called him *The Poet of the Pulpit*; and others, on account of his allegorical illustrations, which he used with greater success than any other Welsh preacher, compared him with John Bunyan. 'Christmas Evans in the pulpit more nearly approached the great Dreamer than any pulpit master of whom we have heard,' writes Paxton Hood. 'Many of his sermons appear to have been long-sustained parables and pictures alive with allegorical delineation of human character.'

The descriptions he unveiled before his congregations were both beautiful and terrifying—they were striking representations that came alive and were easily intelligible to his hearers. He had the power to make the Bible live and move, to reproduce biblical events in modern garb, to embody and personify, to recount imaginary conversations between characters to illustrate his chosen theme. With 'a genius for observing people and places and characteristics', he presented them to his congregations in a lively and dramatic form. 'His best-known sermons are really dramas—comedies and tragedies with Christmas Evans himself as playwright and actor.'

It has rightly been said that he possessed an overflow of imagination, which meant that he often described everything and everyone in his stories down to the smallest detail. 'Thus Nicodemus was not merely a man of the Pharisees, a ruler of the Jews, but Evans gave him a flowing white beard, a wealth of snow-white hair and a purple robe; and described him making his way furtively at midnight through wind and driving rain to the upper room at Jerusalem.' Occasionally his pictures lacked taste and refinement, but for boldness of creation, for deep feeling and fancy, for forcefulness of detail they were unique and unequalled by any of his contemporaries.

At times his fancy, like a high-spirited racehorse, ran riot and was not disciplined with sufficient sobriety or judgement. He took his pictures too far, working out his illustrations and similes 'to rags and tatters' until they bordered on the extravagant, even the ridiculous, although the sheer realness and unction of the preacher kept the truth firmly in view.

Surprisingly Christmas Evans did not employ much physical movement when preaching. At the beginning of his career he attempted a few strokes and motions in way of actions, but they were awkward and clumsy, and his friends advised him to abandon them. Consequently he only used to stretch forth a hand occasionally or point a finger or shrug his shoulders or shake his head, gesticulations that were always easy, appropriate and forcible; and which, if not graceful, at least complemented his manner of speaking.

His powerful voice, tender rather than harsh, did not possess the variation of tone common to many Welsh preachers, nor did he vary the speed of his utterance; rather he 'spoke right on, his words following in rapid succession one after the other, as if there were a crowd of them at the gates pressing on for utterance, until the flow of speech was amazing and astounding to the hearer. Sometimes the preacher would shout at a high pitch of voice, somewhat approaching a scream.'

Christmas Evans has been criticised, and in many cases rightly so, for his use, or over-use, of humour in the pulpit. He had a very keen natural tendency to humour and of seeing and portraying the ridiculous, and with it he used to send congregations into hysterics. He possessed a satirical laugh and the ability to flash suddenly before his hearers a gleam of something absurd. At times his use of humour, though enjoyed by many, bordered on indecorum in the house of God, and brought too much of the theatre into the place of worship. This tendency in our preacher, a defect certainly, was nonetheless one of the reasons for his popularity, and although he tried to keep it in check, he allowed it more rein than other Welsh preachers.

There were times before preaching when he experienced a kind of 'stage fright', which so gripped him that he was reluctant to stand before a congregation. Sometimes, if he felt he did not have the congregation's sympathy, he could not continue with his sermon. Once, when he was announced to preach in his old neighbourhood of Llandysul, 'and expecting some persons to be present whom he knew would be disposed to question his deliverances, he was so unnerved by the prospect, that he could not be prevailed upon to fulfil his engagement, unless a local brother minister would go and *stand by him*'.

At times, as a result of these panic attacks, he utterly failed in his preaching, much to his own dismay. If he was expected to preach again in the same neighbourhood after a failure, all the powers and authorities could not persuade him to re-appear. One day, after preaching very unsatisfactorily in the morning, and being announced to appear again in the afternoon, he escaped to a farm house which he well knew, 'but by the time he reached there, every man, woman and child had gone to hear Christmas Evans! And to complete his adversity, having got into the farmyard, he was there imprisoned by a fierce dog, who would not allow the preacher to escape until the family returned *after* the service was over, to witness and to help him out of his predicament!'

However, these failures and weaknesses, common to every public speaker, were far outweighed by the gifts and authority he possessed, causing many to speak of him as 'the greatest preacher God has ever given to Wales'.

Select bibliography

The Dictionary of National Biography (London: Oxford University Press, 1956–1960).

The Dictionary of Welsh Biography Down to 1940 (London: 1959).

T. M. Bassett, *The Welsh Baptists* (Swansea: Ilston House, 1977).

Joseph Cross, *Sermons and Memoirs of Christmas Evans* (New York: Leary & Getz, 1856, reprinted Grand Rapids: Kregel Publications, 1986).

David Davies, *Echoes from the Welsh Hills* (London: Passmore and Alabaster, 1888, reprinted Stoke-on-Trent: Tentmaker Publications, 2000).

John Davies, *A History of Wales* (London: Penguin Books, 1994).

J. Davis (Translator), *Sermons on Various Subjects by Rev. Christmas Evans* (Beaver, 1837).

J. Davis, *History of the Welsh Baptists* (Pittsburgh: D. M. Hogan, 1835, reprinted Gallatin: Church History Research & Archives, 1982).

J. Davis, *Memoir of the Rev. Christmas Evans, A Minister of the Gospel in the Principality of Wales* (Mount Pleasant: J. Davis & S. Siegfried, 1840).

D. M. Evans, *Christmas Evans: A Memoir, The Bunyan Library, vol. IX* (London: J. Heaton & Son, 1863).

Paxton Hood, *Christmas Evans: The Preacher of Wild Wales* (London: Hodder & Stoughton, 1888).

Geraint H. Jenkins, *The Foundations of Modern Wales: Wales 1642–1780* (Oxford: Oxford University Press, 1993).

Owen Jones, *Some of the Great Preachers of Wales* (Passmore & Alabaster, 1885, reprinted Clonmel: Tentmaker Publications, 1995).

D. Densil Morgan, *Christmas Evans and the New Nonconformity* (Christmas Evans a'r Ymneilltuaeth Newydd), (Llandysul: Gomer Press, 1991).

D. Densil Morgan, *The Development of the Baptist Movement in Wales Between 1714 and 1815* (Unpublished Thesis, University of Oxford, 1986).

David Phillips, *Memoir of the Life, Labors and Extensive Usefulness of the Rev. Christmas Evans* (New York: M. W. Dodd, 1843).

E. Ebrard Rees, *Christmas Evans* (London: The Kingsgate Press, c.1935).

Thomas Rees, *History of Protestant Nonconformity in Wales* (London: John Snow and Co., 1883).

David Rhys Stephen, *Memoirs of the Late Christmas Evans of Wales* (London: Aylott and Jones, 1847).

R. E. Williams (Translator), *The Allegories of Christmas Evans* (Aberdare: G. M. Evans, 1899).

About Day One:

Day One's threefold commitment:

- To be faithful to the Bible, God's inerrant, infallible Word;
- To be relevant to our modern generation;
- To be excellent in our publication standards.

I continue to be thankful for the publications of Day One. They are biblical; they have sound theology; and they are relative to the issues at hand. The material is condensed and manageable while, at the same time, being complete—a challenging balance to find. We are happy in our ministry to make use of these excellent publications.

JOHN MACARTHUR, PASTOR-TEACHER, GRACE COMMUNITY CHURCH, CALIFORNIA

It is a great encouragement to see Day One making such excellent progress. Their publications are always biblical, accessible and attractively produced, with no compromise on quality. Long may their progress continue and increase!

JOHN BLANCHARD, AUTHOR, EVANGELIST AND APOLOGIST

Visit our web site for more information and to request a free catalogue of our books.

www.dayone.co.uk

John Rogers—
sealed with blook

TIM SHENTON

144 PAGES, ILLUSTRATED PAPERBACK

978–1–84625–084–2

We in the west sorely need to craft a theology of martyrdom—it would put backbone into our proclamation and living, and help us remember brothers and sisters going through fiery trials even today in other parts of the world. Remembering men like John Rogers is a great help in the development of such a theology. From the foreword by Michael Haykin, Principal and Professor of Church History and Reformed Spirituality, Toronto Baptist Seminary, Toronto, Ontario

'Tim Shenton has produced yet another well-documented, gripping biography of a real hero of faith—John Rogers (d. 1555), renowned biblical editor and first Marian martyr. Follow Rogers's fascinating career from Antwerp to Germany, and back again to England, where he was arrested, remained steadfast under intense interrogation, and paid the ultimate price for confessing Christ. This is a great book about an important epigone; hopefully, Rogers will no longer be marginalized! Highly recommended for teenagers and adults.'
—*Joel R Beeke, Puritan Reformed Theological Seminary, Grand Rapids, Michigan*

John Rogers—
sealed with blood
The story of the first Protestant
martyr of Mary Tudor's reign

Tim Shenton

'Shenton weaves a brilliant tapestry from original sources and introduces the reader to many compelling and complex personalities. Well-proportioned in its emphasis, this history will be a vital contribution to studies of Protestant martyrs in Queen Mary's reign.'
—*Randall J. Pederson, co-author of 'Meet the Puritans'*

TIM SHENTON

192 PAGES, ILLUSTRATED PAPERBACK

978–1–90308–770–1

Forgotten heroes of revival

Five men of the 18th century evangelical awakening

The forgotten heroes of revival described here were men of passion. Their deep love for Jesus Christ and for the souls of their listeners enabled them to stand strong through the storms of persecution and to preach a message that didn't only address the mind with truth, but reached right into the hearts of their hearers. As they proclaimed the Word of Life, it shook their congregations—it stirred them—and many were saved! Read about James Rouquet, George Thomson, Captain Jonathan Scott, David Simpson and Thomas Pentycross.

Tim Shenton is the head teacher of St Martin's School and an elder at Lansdowne Baptist Church, Bournemouth. He is married with two daughters. He has researched and written extensively on church history, specializing in the eighteenth and nineteenth centuries. Among his works published by Day One are *Forgotten heroes of revival, Our perfect God, Opening up 1 Thessalonians* and an expositional commentary on the prophet Habakkuk.

COLIN HAMER

160PP, ILLUSTRATED PAPERBACK

978-1-84625-083-5

Anne Boleyn
One short life that changed
the English-speaking world

Colin Hamer

Day One

Anne Boleyn, twenty years old, stepped onto the shore at Dover in the winter of 1521 after several years abroad. She had been sent to France to assimilate French culture, and had used the time well. She was all set to make a big impression at the Tudor court—and did, capturing the heart of Henry VIII.

But this woman, who was in the grave by the age of thirty-six and on the throne of England for only three years, provokes strong reactions from many. Was she an immoral woman who seduced Henry away from his rightful wife for the advancement of family and personal gain? In this well-researched, fresh look at Anne, Colin Hamer sets her in her context as a young woman who had come to true faith in Christ, and shows the impact for good she made from her position of influence, an impact we still benefit from today.

Colin Hamer is currently chairman of a charity that works with the homeless and other vulnerable groups. Following his graduation from Liverpool University in 1972 with BA (Hons), he spent a short time teaching then pursued a business career for more than twenty-five years. He has been an elder at Grace Baptist Church, Astley, Manchester, for twenty years.

He and his wife Lois have two adult children. His first book, *Being a Christian Husband—a biblical perspective*, was published by Evangelical Press in 2005.

'In this fascinating biography of her short life, Colin Hamer skillfully shows how God prepared Anne for this important work and used her to bring Reformed truth into the powerhouse of England.'
—*Kath Dredge, Further Education tutor and manager of Hall Green BookPoint, Haworth*

'Colin Hamer's Anne Boleyn is as exciting as fiction as it carefully makes its way through the historical and religious complexities of Henry VIII's England.'
—*David B. Calhoun, Professor of Church History at Covenant Theological Seminary, St Louis, Missouri*